I heard Laura speak at the United Nations, and I instantly knew that I had to ask her to be part of my business. With her expertise and guidance, this book will not only propel your business to new heights but pinpoint those areas of your business you know need a stronger focus.

—Jenevieve Brewer, Founder, Jenevieve Brewer Talent Management, LLC

This book will transform your life.

—Matt Williams, Partner, Wind Dancer Films

Every money manager needs to talk to Laura. Laura is the catalyst to make profitable deals happen.

—Caroline Abramo, CEO and Founder, Pana Consulting, LLC

In politics, campaigns don't usually win or lose, they run out of money and time. So it's important to implement the strategies set forth in Laura's new book and ASK.

—Rob Cole, Founder and CEO, in the Field Global, Specializing in Media and Political Campaigns.

As a teenager, when you want to make something happen in school, sports, friendships, or anything else, you have to ask. Laura's approach helps you learn the necessity of asking in the best way possible.

—Caroline Paske Baulig

Laura has always impressed me with her energy and her passion for helping people to achieve their goals. She has been a student of the process of asking throughout her career, and this book lets you in on her secrets of THE ASK. Laura is the master asker.

—Robert E. Wahlers, CFRE, VP of Development, Hackensack Meridian Health and Adjunct Professor, Columbia University MS in Nonprofit Management

Hallelujah, a female expert on asking! Every conversation with Laura delivers clear next steps for my financial gain, success in my career, and personal fulfillment. I'm living the life of my dreams supported with the power of THE ASK.

—*K. Marsden, Managing Partner, Touchpoint Strategies*

The most invaluable perspective I learned from Laura is that when you remove the fear around asking for things you need, you remove the barriers between you and the success you and your business deserve. This book is a must read for anyone wanting to get to the next level personally or professionally.

—*Ashleigh Young, Founder of Power Hour Consulting, LLC*

Asking for help in our self-sufficient society, even if desperately needed, is incredibly difficult and borders on impossible for military families. The guidance in this well-crafted book allows the reader to put "the ask" in the proper context and thereby create a clear path connecting those with a real need to those with a viable solution.

—*John Pray, leader of an organization dedicated to supporting military families in need*

Laura has transformed the way we approach fundraising and inspires us to follow our passion with conviction. She has helped us to build our confidence as an organization, and we see, feel, and experience the results of her philosophy. Laura Fredricks rocks!

—*Angelina Fiordellisi, Founding Artistic Director, Cherry Lane Theatre*

THE ASK is important to my business because it has taught me how to ASK for what we need to continue giving caregivers the care they deserve.

—*Sherri Reed, Founder and CEO, Sanctuary for Life*

*the*ASK

Laura Fredricks, JD

*the*ASK

for BUSINESS,
for PHILANTHROPY,
for EVERYDAY LIVING

WILEY

To anyone who needs to ASK for what you want, need, and deserve; this is for YOU.

Contents

Preface

THE ASK IS YOUR *GATEWAY TO YOUR SUC-CESS in every aspect of your life.* Whether you want a more fulfilling personal life, a better and more high-paying job, more sales, or more money for your nonprofit, it all comes down to THE ASK.

As "The Expert on the ASK," I know this book will transform the way you will make any ask in your life. That's a start. But it will also transform the way you approach life. *When you ask you empower.* You empower not only yourself, but also anyone you encounter. When you ask, your confidence, your energy, and your determination and focus draw people toward you. They want to learn more about you—your passions and your products, projects, and programs—and, in turn, they *want* to help you.

Whenever someone asks me what I do, I say "I help people, businesses, and nonprofits raise money—and more of it." The very next thing everyone says to me is "Gee, I need to speak to you." Why? Of course they probably need to raise money for something, but they genuinely want to know *how to ask.* They know they need to learn how to do it because it is a missing piece whose absence limits their personal or professional *growth.*

I have an unstoppable passion to teach and share my asking talent, and it started many years ago. My journey began as a civil-litigation attorney working for the state attorney general's office in

Philadelphia, Pennsylvania. I was winning practically all my cases on cross-examination, which was great. Later on, I looked back and discovered why I had won them all on cross-examination. After all, as a 26-year old deputy attorney general, I thought that that was my job and it was supposed to happen. Looking back with a much more mature and practical eye, I realized I was *asking* the right questions. I quickly learned the power of asking the right questions at the right time. That was the difference between captivating a judge or jury and persuading them to side with my case or losing them and losing the case.

Eight years later, feeling total burnout after working on 162 cases, I transitioned from law to philanthropy. I was creating my own formulas for how to raise big gifts with my ask techniques and breaking every fundraising record for the large universities and the major hospital where I worked. All along, I was writing books on my step-by-step process for asking for money, because no one had put *organization, structure,* and *focus* on an area that had been largely left to chance, luck, and time. My legal background prepared me to bear down on the facts; be a superior listener; and prepare, prepare, and prepare for any and all responses to my asks. I started my own consulting firm, sharing my ask practice with each of my clients. Again, every organization's fundraising totals skyrocketed because they had learned how to ask great questions at the right time and then how to make THE ASK using my techniques. Then it dawned on me that THE ASK is not just for nonprofits, it is for everyone in business and everyday living. So I wrote two books on THE ASK that are international industry go-to guides. For over two decades I traveled the world speaking on THE ASK because I truly believe with every ember I have that THE ASK is the most important, empowering skill that anyone of any age and living anywhere on the planet needs to possess to have the best life possible. I have had teenagers come up to me and say that they needed THE ASK to help them find their voice so that they could speak up to bullies. Seniors would tell me they needed THE ASK so they could have the conversation with their children to help pay for their grandchildren's education. Entrepreneurs of all ages, once they heard what I do, had to know how to ask and get money for their start-ups.

THE ASK is for anyone in the media, politics, fundraising, sales, marketing, insurance, finance, travel, health, wellness, beauty, technology, science, religion, theater, education, arts, and athletics who needs to ask in order to get ahead in life. Not asking is probably the reason why most people experience depression, low self-esteem, weight gain, weight loss, lack of sleep, and problems at work and in their personal relationships. This book will show you step by step how to make your best ask in any area of your life. It will also show you how you can turn around any ask that did not go exactly the way you wanted and get it back on track the way you *do* want it.

This book puts the focus on you as the asker. It starts with the premise that you will be making the ask and that you know whom you want to ask or at least have ideas of whom you can ask. If you need some guidance, tips, and techniques to determine who should make the ask, how to build a pipeline of people you can ask, or how to decide on the right setting for making the ask, I strongly recommend that you first read *THE ASK: How to Ask for Support for Your Nonprofit Cause, Creative Project, or Business Venture* (Fredricks, Jossey Bass, 2010). That will equip you with the knowledge and practical tips you need so that you can get the most from this book.

So what exactly is THE ASK, and why is this book different from previous books, including mine, about this life skill? I have listened carefully for over 25 years to the comments made at my seminars and conferences, and to the scenarios that people have presented me when they needed to ask. I have read all the emails and notes that people sent me about their ask experiences, and I have reflected on the contributions I had made on television, radio, and newspaper interviews on THE ASK. The common theme was that everyone wanted me to expand and highlight THE ASK as a change agent for people's lives. They shared with me that THE ASK frees them from fear of rejection and empowers them to say "I can do this for anything I want at any time." They expressed a feeling of pure joy when they knew in their hearts that they had made the right ask, *regardless of the result.* Their win was that they had made THE ASK, which gave them more self-confidence in every aspect of their lives.

That's what this book is all about. THE ASK is about more than getting what you want. THE ASK is my self-help motivational book for people who have dreams, goals, and a strong desire to have the best and most fulfilling personal and professional life possible. I've taken my previous work on THE ASK and added an off-the-charts new dimension. THE ASK defines what anyone, anywhere needs to do to be successful in any area of their life. You see, this is about much more than getting more money for your nonprofit, getting that higher-paying job, or getting your significant other to do more work around the house. Will THE ASK accomplish those goals? You bet. But it does not end there. THE ASK will change the way you think, the way you approach life, and the way you tackle each goal or challenging event that comes your way. You will have the skills to use as well as the mindset to approach life very differently because you will have the confidence and certainty that you have made the right ask every time. So THE ASK is not just a skill; *it is a lifestyle*.

For many of us, our asks involve some aspect of money. When you think of it *every decision you make in life involves money*. Do you make coffee or buy coffee? Do you drive or take mass transit? Do you sleep in and take a pay cut that day at work? Do you hire a babysitter or stay in Friday night? Do you buy new clothes or alter the ones you have? Do you clean your house or have someone do it for you? I could go on and on, but I know you get my point. Truly every decision you make (and we make dozens of decisions each hour, day, month, and year) involves some aspect of money. This is why I begin Chapter 1 with a focus on tackling the meaning, the values, and the beliefs we place on money.

Many people do not ask because they have a horrible relationship with money. To them it means debt, obligation, depression, loans, alimony, insecurity, and arguments. How can anyone ask if they have a horrible and age-old problem with money? In the initial chapter we work through what I call your "money blockers," those thoughts and sabotaging behaviors that prevent you from having the best relationship with money. Once your money blockers are turned off, you will be clearly focused and convinced that *money is opportunity*. This transitional mindset will allow you to be open for the following steps, which involve learning the essentials before you make your ask.

Chapter 2 walks you through the top 10 reasons why people should ask. The one that heads the list and is the underlying theme of this entire book is *empowerment*. When you ask, you create the greatest sense of self-worth that no one can give you; you give it to yourself when you ask. This will allow you to stand out amongst your peers. It will allow you to become the role model in all your relationships. It will define who you are, what you want, and how you will organize your thoughts and orchestrate your actions on a consistent and seamless basis. I end Chapter 2 with Laura's ASKing mantras, which have served me so well over the years—trust me, they work. They have helped numerous boards, sales teams, families, financial planners, and boyfriends and girl-friends attain and then exceed their professional and personal goals. They will also help you when you are faced with the most challenging and emotionally draining asks.

I always like to anticipate what the reader might be saying after I list the positive effects of THE ASK, because I know there are reasons why people don't ask. In Chapter 3 I list the top 10 reasons why people don't ask and I provide workable solutions to shift your mindset away from negative beliefs. THE ASK needs to have a positive focus at all times. As Grant Cardone in his book *Sell or Be Sold* (Greenleaf Book Group, 2012) says, you need to go on a "negative diet," and I will help you melt away your negative "I can't ask" pounds in this book.

Everyone has the potential to be what I call the Exceptional Asker. How you become that Exceptional Asker depends on the beliefs and values you place on your ask. In Chapter 4 I list the specific traits and values that I aspire to with each and every ask I make. That list has helped me over and over again as well as the people and teams I coach and train. Whether you are a media talent, philanthropist, politician, investor, producer, mom, life-style expert, athlete, teacher, or student I guarantee you need to know, embrace, and demonstrate these qualities. I just love to see the look on people's faces when they realize that they must first *own their ask*. THE ASK is so much more than knowing what you want, making the ask, and then praying for a good result. THE

ASK requires organization, structure, and focus, and it all begins with you. You have to own your ask. Do you believe 100 percent in your ask? If you do not, I promise that you will be disappointed with the result. I share with you in this chapter how you can embrace the core beliefs and traits of the Exceptional Asker as well as set the stage with the essentials you need to know and practice before you ask.

One of the key elements of THE ASK that distinguishes this book from all others is that I make the world of asking *unbelievably simple*. I know that if it is simple, it is doable. However, it is doable only if there is the right preparation. At the heart of THE ASK are my preparation steps. If you take the time to carefully work through and prepare solid answers, you will be doing a victory lap with each ask. In Chapter 4 are my incredibly simple but powerful three questions that come before any ask:

- Why me?
- Why now?
- What will it do?

These are simple questions that anyone needs to ask and answer, particularly if they do not have much time before they make their ask. I walk you through the ways you can answer those questions because they always come up. When you can quickly prepare solid answers to these three questions, you will be that much close to getting a "Yes" answer, and that is exactly where you want to be.

After you have the answers to these three simple questions, you will be ready for my more in-depth preparation for your ask in Chapter 5, which presents my 5-Step Foolproof Method for Any ASK. I created these five steps recently and I've witnessed transformational results. Why? Simply put, *people crave structure*. If there is structure, people have guidance and a path to follow. THE ASK involves much more than blurting out what you want and hoping the other person will blindly say yes. We have all heard of the quick success stories—the off-the-charts investment deal, the billion-dollar merger, and the million-dollar gift. I know all of these took time and strategy to line up the right person, to make the right ask, using the right words, at the right time with countless hours of preparing the answers to any response that might arise. This is why my 5-Step Foolproof Method for Any ASK is so important. With these five steps, which must be done in an exact order, anyone can make the exceptional ask with exceptional results.

Chapter 5 ends with my latest secret and successful tip. THE ASK is nothing more than *two sentences and a question.* This chapter illustrates with real examples of how this technique works and the words you can use so that you do not over-ask your ask. This reduces the time it takes to make your ask and expedites the time it takes to get a positive answer.

Perhaps the question I am asked most often when I train people on how to make THE ASK is: *What are the words I should use?* Many people have in their minds what they would like to say and the concept they want to get across, but they freeze or say some confusing sentences that make their ask awkward and disjointed. Chapter 5 has the answer because my examples give you suggested words to use. Yes indeed, there are certain words that resonate and are more persuasive and inviting that you can use when you make your ask. This chapter reveals those *winning words* to use and explains how to use them.

Some asks do not go the way you planned. This is why I included the section "Was Your Ask Really an ASK?" in Chapter 6. All too often we think we asked, when in fact we really didn't. Many people are under the impression that statements like "I'd like to have more money" or "I have this great new product" are asks when in fact they are not. I show you in this chapter how to turn around the statements we make in business, fundraising, and everyday life and convert them into powerful asks. This leads into "Asking U-Turns" to use when you receive a "No" answer. I show you how a no now does not and will not mean no later and how to keep your ask alive long after your receive the initial no.

We end Chapter 6 with "Five Ways to Turn a Bad Ask into a Win." Sometimes we just asked the wrong person because the person being asked is not the decision maker, we asked at an inopportune time, or you thought you had asked a question when in fact you had not. Chapter 6 will give you words and phrases to avoid that can sabotage your ask. Fear not; I turn those around for you to get you back on track.

All these tips, tools, techniques, and formulas on THE ASK become real and practical in Chapters 7, 8, and 9 where I share stories and illustrate how THE ASK works in business, philanthropy, and everyday living. You will read some familiar and some not-so-familiar scenarios that will highlight and spotlight how you can use THE ASK in your professional and personal life. There is nothing better than a good story to guide you and inspire you to take that leap of faith and ask for what *you know in your heart you deserve*. These stories are special, meaningful, and personal experiences I have had or situations that people have asked me to work out with them. I am most certain after you read them you will identify yourself or project yourself in the same situation and will learn and emerge with confidence to make your ask. That is my wish for you.

I end the book with Chapter 10, "The Hardest Asks You Will Ever Make." I truly believe that the *hardest asks are the ones you ask yourself*. How do you ask for help, forgiveness, acceptance, patience, strength, faith, love, guidance, inner peace, or more fun? In Chapter 10 I explain why these personal asks are so hard to make and how you can get beyond your trepidation. I know that it is one thing to write about THE ASK, but it is another to live and learn from it.

I saved what I feel is the best for last. Chapter 10 ends with *the hardest asks I have ever made of myself*. You will have to wait until the end of the book to see how these asks transformed my life and made me the most ecstatic and grateful person on the planet. It pulls together all the themes, mantras, tools, tips, and advice I share throughout the book and ends with my story to inspire you.

This book will change your life and you will be amazed by how simple, seamless, and successful asking can be. Let's get that life you dreamed of and make it happen right now. Let's unveil THE ASK together and watch the magic unfold.

Introduction

WELCOME TO MY BOOK—my brand new book—which I am most certain will change the way you approach life because *you asked*. Now, I have written other books on this topic but this book is *completely new*—new techniques, steps, mantras, and stories, and best of all it has *more than* 175 different ways, with sample dialogues, to make your ask. Whatever you need to ask for, this book will show you how to do it and even supply the words to use. I've saved the best for last in the final chapter—the hardest asks you will ever make—and they may surprise you!

I was driven to write this book, and honestly it took me far less time to write than I had anticipated. Every day someone would ask me, *How do I get*: a doctor to give me more options for my condition? my children to get off their cell phones and help around the house? my significant other to agree to retire at the same time? my boss to give me the promotion I deserve? my friends to spend the money and come to my destination wedding? my cousin to invest in my new company? my co-workers to support my charity event? that vacation package upgrade without spending more money? Well, the answers to ALL these questions are right here in this book because I cover it all and in every category—business, philanthropy, and everyday needs. THE ASK will not only show you how to ask, but it will also show you how you can make *an exceptional ask every time*. You will have no fear, no hesitation, and no guessing how you should make your ask. THE ASK will give you all the organization, structure, and focus you need to make any ask.

Many people have asked me how I reached this point and combine all my experiences as a journalist, attorney, fundraiser, speaker, and author, and roll that into becoming the CEO and founder of THE ASK. So I thought I'd share a very entertaining story of my journey and the path to THE ASK.

It was my last year of law school, right before graduation, when friends and even my mother said "Why don't you go see this woman, Peggy? She will tell you about your past and predict what you will do in the future." In other words, a psychic. Everyone was *raving* about Peggy so I thought, "Why not? I have nothing to lose." I had my job all set, clerking for an appellate judge for two years, and then I would go on to a fabulous, high-paying job at a select law firm.

So off I go to see Peggy. I played it *very* cool, not saying a word and trying not to reveal anything that would tip her off about me. I was wearing basic brown and no jewelry. The first thing Peggy did was "read my aura," where she could see the dominant colors surrounding me. She said "You are surrounded by bright yellow, which means you have abundant energy." She got that one right. I've been known to exhaust and outlast my friends and family with unbridled energy in any event, any conversation, anywhere, and at any time! Next she said, "And you have brilliant green around you, meaning you will be surrounded by money all your life." Well, rock and roll! That was exactly what I needed to hear. After all, I had mega law school loans to pay off, starting in three months.

She then started reading my cards and what she said next devastated me. She said, "Whatever you have been studying or whatever you are doing now or will do in the next two years you will *not* be doing the rest of your life." I'm sure I did not contain my surprised look, or my dilated eyes, or my gasp. All I could think was, "I'm about to graduate law school, I've invested three *long* years of my life and I'm *not* going to be practicing law?"

She continued to flip more cards one by one and then defiantly put her right index finger on one card and said, "See there? It is the Scales of Justice." Well, now I felt better. We were getting back on track to law. Maybe I would be a Supreme Court Justice. That sounded good to me I could definitely live with that idea. I began to think this whole ordeal may not be so bad.

"The Scales of Justice is in between the Ten of Cups card, representing family, and the Ten of Pentacles card, representing wealth," Peggy said. "This means your life's work will be helping families be more balanced, and probably about money."

I don't have a finance degree and, in fact, I took one micro economics class in college and almost failed it. My life has been dedicated to words, not numbers. I'm just a journalist on her way to help a judge write his law opinions. I'm sunk.

The very last thing Peggy said to me was "From everything I see, you are the real Don Quixote. You know, the character in Miguel de Cervantes' novel who traveled on his horse from village to village in search of people in need. Like Don Quixote, you are a *questor*. But instead, you will be traveling from city to city and your quest will be to help people. I see so many families that need your help, and they have so many money worries."

That was in 1983. I walked away thinking, "Well, that was entertaining at best," and went about my path. I did clerk for the appellate judge and then went on to practice civil litigation for the State Attorney General's Office in Philadelphia, Pennsylvania, for seven years. Maybe Peggy got the timeline wrong. But in the middle of my sixth year at the Attorney General's Office I was getting absolute burnout. I had dozens of cases assigned to me and the reward for winning a case was getting a brand new one. My "unbridled energy" had left me and I was exhausted. At the time, I was very active with the Philadelphia Bar Association and they had a foundation that raised and distributed money to community legal services such as Women Against Abuse, Juvenile Law Center, and Legal Clinic for the Disabled. They asked me to be the director of development to help them raise money and distribute funds to these legal community organizations. This is how I transitioned from law to philanthropy. So there I was, raising money for families in need of legal services. Peggy's words surfaced, *families, money, me?*

And so the journey unfolds. I spent the next two decades raising millions of dollars for nonprofits such as the Deborah Heart and Lung Hospital (from grateful patients), Temple University, and Pace University (from alumni, and their families). Afterwards, I started my own consulting business with amazing groups like the American Heart Association, the Central Park Conservancy, Planned Parenthood, and Operation Homefront, working with these organizations to raise unprecedented amounts of money.

While I am happily raising money, I discovered that *asking* for money came very easily to me but was torturous, painful, and uncomfortable to many. I developed a whole new organization, structure, and focus on how to ask for money and wrote two books on THE ASK. I started speaking internationally on THE ASK traveling to Russia, Australia, Italy, Mexico, and the Netherlands, and teaching it at several Ivy League universities and at international conferences, helping not only nonprofits but also businesses and individuals on how to ask for money, the right way with amazing results. Don Quixote indeed, except I travel by train, plane, or rental car.

Throughout this entire journey, I had the privilege of working with people to fulfill their philanthropic dreams; to start or escalate their businesses; to ask for a raise, a promotion, a new job title; or simply to ask for what they need and deserve in their personal or professional life. But before I could get them these results, I discovered that many people had crazy definitions and relationships with money that were taking a toll on their personal and professional lives *and their health*.

All these experiences brought me to this point in time that drove me to write this brand new book on THE ASK. As you will see, *every* decision you make in life involves money. How and even *if* you ask depends on your attitudes, beliefs, and values about money. In the past, I did focus much of my time, my practice, and my passion to help people raise money but I found that while THE ASK can help you ask for money, it does much more than get you the money you want. THE ASK is empowerment on every level. It empowers you to break out and away from everything that has held you back from asking for whatever you need *and deserve.* THE ASK, this book, will change your life because you are in the driver's seat and you can get what you want and deserve—because you made that exceptional ask. THE ASK is your life's manual that will free you to have anything you can dream.

What Will THE ASK Do for You?

1

What Is THE ASK?

T

HE ASK IS THE NAME OF THE SUREFIRE way that you can have the most fulfilling personal and professional life and find abundant success wherever you go. Who would not want that? The answer may surprise you. There are many people who know they need to ask in order to get what they want, but they talk themselves out of it, convince themselves they can get it without asking, or worse yet, have a conversation in their head in which the other person will say no before they even ask. All this time and energy is wasted on fruitless conversations and mindsets that result only in your not getting what you want. Depression sets in, self-confidence diminishes, and we settle for what we have, not what we can achieve on the greatest scale.

The number-one reason people do not get what they want in life is quite simple: *They have not asked!* This is a horrible way to live life. Now, let's shift this mindset around. The number-one reason people do not *give* is they have not been asked. That represents real opportunity. People are not going to give you a raise, a hotel room upgrade, better theater seats, an explanation about your bill, a charitable gift, more clients, feedback on your business venture, extra help around the house, or more time with your significant other unless you ask.

I have spent over three decades of my life analyzing, practicing, and perfecting THE ASK in law, philanthropy, business, and everyday living. I can proudly tell you that I am the first to put such *organization, structure, and focus* on THE ASK. This is the theme you will read throughout this book. THE ASK is not random, it is not chance, and it certainly is not luck. THE ASK is not asking dozens of people, hoping someone will give you a yes. We have all heard of the quick successes, the billion-dollar gift, the unprecedented acquisition, and the million-dollar start-up that leads us to believe that we don't really have to ask for great success. If we work hard it will come to us. *I assure you that every success you hear about had many great asks along the way.*

I have the utmost certainty that everyone has the ability to make exceptional asks; they just need to know how and then see real results. This is why I've written this book. I put the world of asking into simple, easy-to-follow steps, keeping in mind that many people don't want to—or, as I have heard numerous times—"hate to ask." For example, a friend of mine is an enormously successful television producer and screenwriter. He told me that he can do anything, but he can't ask for money. I was blown away. I know he has asked for more time to write his scripts, for different actors, for different set designs, and for actors to use a better way to deliver his lines. He is like the hundreds of people who come to my seminars and conferences all buttoned up in their resistance to ask for money.

So I asked him, "What is it about asking for money that you differentiate from any other ask you make many times throughout the day?" He was a little taken aback and said, "What do you mean?" So I shared with him that he makes asks all the time, effortlessly and flawlessly, because he knows he needs something and asking will get him what he needs. Without his asks, he will be unsuccessful in his business because he will have to settle for a show, an actor, or a design that is not up to his standards. He said "Yeah, but that's not asking for money." This is where so many people make this huge demarcation between making "easy asks" and asking for money. I gave him the advice that is so important for everyone to embrace. *Every decision you make in life involves money.* In his case I showed him that asking for a better actor meant paying for a better actor and asking for more time to write his script would cause his producers to be delayed in receiving their money from the sponsors; as for better set designs and more props, they all cost extra. So, in essence, he was asking for money without using the word "money." This was a huge revelation for him. While he still has a hard time getting the words out to ask for a specific amount, he at least has a new awareness that he really has done this before and needs to practice asking for cash.

THE ASK is not just for people in finance or philanthropy. THE ASK is for everyone who needs something from someone else or needs something from themselves. THE ASK is for whatever you want. If you need to ask for help, clarity, insight, or feedback, my techniques and tips will show you *how* to ask as well as the words to use to get real results. That's as simple as it gets. If you need to get into your first-choice graduate school, you need to ask the admissions director. If you want your child to have a different position on the team, you need to ask the coach. If you need to stay home with your significant other this holiday and not spend it with the relatives, you need to ask your sweetheart. If you need more work to make extra money, you need to ask your boss for extra projects. If you want to know the alternatives available to you to address a medical need, you need to ask your doctor. The list of asks is endless.

The reality is that most people do not know exactly what they want. They crave better relationships, more time off, a better body, more sleep, better health care, more education and training, more spiritual guidance, more retirement money, a vacation home, time to read a book or to be creative, or time and money to give to a worthy cause. When they fail to ask for it, the result is the hollow feeling that says they are not as good as they can be. That's no way to live your life. THE ASK can and will show you how you will feel *empowered and energized* because you made the ask—you didn't just wish you had asked.

Now you see how THE ASK *is vital to your life and your happiness in your life.* Yes, you could settle for what you have now, but how off-the-charts amazing would it be if you asked *with confidence* for anything you want and desire? I'm here to tell you THE ASK works, and it will work for you once you read this book and then practice and apply my techniques. I hope the stories that are woven throughout this book will resonate with you as you identify similar situations, words, behaviors, mindsets, challenges, and experiences. I hope you find THE ASK so rewarding that you share it with your family, your network, your colleagues, and of course your friends.

A couple who are very close friends of mine were sharing my previous book *THE ASK: How to ASK for Your Nonprofit Cause,*

Creative Project, or Business Venture. This book was on their bedroom nightstand. They told me that each night they tried to hop into bed to be the first to grab my book and read it. He was working for a large insurance company and had not had a raise in four years. She was a therapist and need more clients. They didn't just read the book; they put it to their own personal test. He had a meeting with his boss and followed my "three steps to asking for a raise." Not only did he get it on the spot, but he kicked himself for not asking sooner. She followed my "how to ask friends and family" for more business. She now has a waiting list of prospective clients.

This book is my previous book on steroids. I have more experiences to apply, more phrases to use, and more life lessons to share. Are you ready *to just ask*?

WHAT DOES MONEY MEAN TO YOU?

I was teaching a class on THE ASK. I designed this class so that the morning session would cover my methods on how to ask, when to ask, where to ask, who should ask, how to prepare for the responses, how to close, how to follow up, and how to manage expectations. The second half of the class is devoted to what I call "Laura's practice studio." It is the students' time to shine and practice their ask. One student plays the asker and the other the person being asked. I have the students arrange the chairs and table in the way that is most comfortable for them to make their ask. A young, bright but scared-to-death student gets up and places the chairs opposite each other with a large table in between them. She makes her ask and says, "I would like you to support scholarships at our private school." Her ask did not have a dollar amount or a timeline for making the scholarship.

The class then had the opportunity to share what they liked about the ask and how it could be improved. They said that she needed to ask for a specific amount; otherwise the person being asked cannot make a decision about supporting the scholarship. The person would simply not know the amount to consider. I said that she needed to add *when* she wanted the scholarship. Timing is important because the person you ask needs to know when you need what you're asking for. I also asked her why she placed a table in between them during the exercise. She said the distance from the person she was asking gave her more confidence and without it she would be too close.

I asked her why she felt she needed this distance from the person she was going to ask. After all, when you make the ask, you need to convey that this is very important to you and that you are there 100 percent to help the person make this important decision. She said she was not a fan of freestyle role-playing and preferred writing scripts and reading from them. She continued that asking is way out of her comfort zone. She thinks of herself as a "giver," not a "taker." She will give before she takes. She held her head high and said quite firmly that her family raised her with pride and strong values. I was taken by her honesty, but I had to get to the core of this, because being a giver all your life will not allow you the breathing room to make an ask for money. I felt that if I did not at least try to gently uncover her views about money, she would struggle with asking for money all her life.

So at that very moment I did what I love to do with each person who tells me they cannot ask for money. I simply asked, "When you ask for money, what comes up for you?" She didn't know what to say at first, but then it all came out. She was a young child playing with her siblings and cousins who were younger than she was. Her uncle told them all that if they played quietly he would give them a dollar. At the end of the afternoon, her uncle came in and gave each of the children a dollar *except* her and told her she did not earn it or deserve it. The class went dead silent. This memory, filled with shame and guilt and low self-esteem, literally pushed her to identify herself as the *giver*, not the *taker*. So for her, to ask for money is a shameful event, and she becomes the taker.

This student is not unlike the screenwriter friend that I wrote about previously in this chapter and not unlike many, many people who have a very difficult time asking for money. I have taught, coached, and trained people all over the world on how to ask for money and more of it. There is not one stereotypical person, whatever their age, sex, profession, geographic location, or lifestyle who has an easier or more difficult time with asking for money. It comes down to one factor and one factor alone: *What does money mean to you?* This is not the same question as: *Do you have money?* or *Were you raised comfortably with money, or did you have no money at all?* I begin every session with that question. In the answer, I am looking for the values and beliefs each person attaches to money. It always falls in two areas: the positive and the not so positive. The positive folks view money as:

- Power
- Freedom
- Choices
- Change
- Opportunity
- Selection
- Control
- Independence
- Expression
- Security
- Creativity
- Education
- Health

On the opposite side, money can mean:

- Debt
- Obligation
- Loans
- Insecurity
- No retirement
- Headaches
- Divorce
- Alimony
- No health care
- No choices
- Depression
- Insecurity
- Low self-esteem
- Failure

These are complicated feelings with emotionally laden stories underneath them, and they come up when you ask. Many people try to tell me they are just fine with money, but when they practice asking for it, I can see right through them. My job is to make you 100 percent secure about money before you ask for it. Remember: *Any ask you make has a money implication.* Even if you are not asking for a dollar amount, your ask will involve money. Consider the following list of what money can mean, and you will have a new appreciation that money is embedded in every ask you make. Money can:

- Define your stature in life.
- Determine your success or lack of success.
- Be the reason you stick with your job.

- Determine when and if you retire.
- Be a factor in when and where your children or grand-children go to school.
- Set the limits of what you give to your family during your lifetime and through your will.
- Govern how much you spend and borrow.
- Be the deciding factor in where you live and where you have a vacation home.
- Make you reflect on whether you made the right choices in your life.
- Govern how much you will inherit.
- Determine how much you can spend and save on a monthly basis.
- Govern how and where you spend your free time.
- Give you confidence in deciding whether to start a new business venture or to hold off until later.
- Be a factor in your health care and insurance coverage.
- Play a positive or challenging role in your relationships.
- Bring your family closer together or tear them apart.
- Motivate or discourage you to be like others who have more than you.
- Free you to take risks or prevent you from making changes.
- Determine how much you can invest.
- Determine how much or how little you can give to charity.
- Keep you up at night.
- Be the source of arguments, tension, and unspoken resentment.
- Be the most stressful topic of conversation.
- Cause you to gain or lose weight.
- Affect what you eat and where you eat.
- Influence the time you spend to be creative or to relax.
- Keep you from being spiritually connected.
- Release you from worry and responsibilities.

- Govern how and where you exercise.
- Touch every aspect of your life and the lives of those around you.

Money does touch every aspect of your life, which is why it is so important that you come to terms with how you feel about money and how it influences your comfort level in asking for money.

Money Is Opportunity

The best way I can help you is to encourage you to embrace one small but powerful mindset: *money is opportunity*. If you can try and work out your thoughts and beliefs that anything and everything you ask for will lead to an opportunity, you are home free. Any ask is an opportunity—an opportunity for you to share, grow, prosper, thrive, be a leader, teach, trail-blaze, and, yes, reach the success you envision. Money represents opportunity for the person you are asking. Their opportunities are that they can work with you, share expertise, give, invest, learn, bring about change, make an impact on the lives of those around them, bring joy, and enrich the lives of their community, state, nation, and the world. Believing that asking for money represents anything but opportunity will severely diminish your ability to ask for money. Trust me; I have seen this in real life, from mothers who want to get back into the workforce and financial executives who can't take their business to the next level. Money is opportunity. Embrace it, make it your mantra, and push away any other thought that comes creeping in that sets you up for doubt and failure.

What Does Money Mean to the Person You Are Asking?

We tackled the first side of the equation by focusing on *you*, the asker. Let's take this to the next step and find out what money means to the person you are asking and why it should matter? I was working in development at a university, and one of my donors was a very wealthy man. He had made his fortune in real estate. He had gone to the university and so had his children, who were now adults and doing well in their respective fields. At the time I was assigned to work with him, he was making yearly gifts of $1,000. Now those were great gifts, but when you see the potential of what he had and what he could give, it seemed way off. I took him to every basketball game (and the season, as you know, is very long) and gave him special seats to all our events, which he enjoyed. He met and knew very well the president of our university, the trustees, the dean of his school, and the current students. Every time we asked him to make a larger gift, he would give us $1,000. We asked him for an outright gift, a planned gift, a gift of insurance, a trust, an annuity, and he would give us $1,000.

I thought it was me and that I was doing something wrong. That had to be the only explanation. One day we were seated together at a luncheon, and I don't know what came over me but I turned to him and asked, "When you give the university $1,000 does it feel like a million dollars?" Now I'm thinking to myself I'm definitely going to get fired. He answered, "Yes." I said to myself, "OK, Laura, now what do I do?" I asked him "If it is OK with you, can you share with me why?" What he said to me was incredible and a life lesson for me. He said to me that his mother told him to be a saver. He saw her go through World War I and the stock market crash and her words echoed in his head every day. While he had more than enough money for his family, he just couldn't give more because "he may need it." And there it was. The core reason why he could not give more was that it was impossible for him to do it. He is the exemplary *saver*, and there was nothing I could do, say, or offer that would put a dent into his emotional attachment and his *will to save*.

I was fortunate that this experience came early in my career, because, from that moment on, I have always navigated my way to finding out what money means to the person I want to ask. This, as you can imagine, is not an easy task. You could blurt out, "Hey, I'm about to ask you for money, but before I do what does it mean to you?" That would not get you very far. But I do have a tried-and-true way you can find out without using the word *money*. Whenever I am stuck and need an answer, *open-ended questions win the day*. So here are some questions you can ask before you make your ask. If you want to ask for a philanthropic gift or for someone to be on your board or to volunteer for your organization (each ask has money implications), ask this question: *What is your first memory of when you knew the importance of giving back?*

Nowhere in this question will you find the word *money*, and yet it will get to the heart of how a person feels about money. You will hear responses that generally fit three categories: home, religion, or education. Many people learn the importance of giving back or volunteering from their parents, siblings, relatives at home; through their religious practices; or through teachers and mentors in school. I have heard stories that people learned to give back when they went trick-or-treating on Halloween for UNICEF, served in a soup kitchen with their family during Thanksgiving, baked pies and cookies for a church or school fundraiser, saw a movie that moved them to volunteer, or watched their cousin give money to someone who was homeless and had no place to go. The stories you will hear are incredible, and they will draw you closer to the person you will eventually ask for money. It is so important that you know how they feel about money before you ask.

This applies to business ventures and everyday living as well. If you want to ask someone to invest in your start-up business, you could ask, "*Have you invested in other ventures, and what motivates you to be an investor?*"

Nowhere do you see the word *money*, but their answer will be so revealing. If the answer includes an exciting and rewarding investment, they will tell you how great it was to take something from concept to market and what a thrill it was to be part of a successful venture. Investors are not just people with money who take chances. For the most part they are careful and strategic planners, and if you know that, you can tailor your ask. For example, your ask might sound like this:

> *You shared with me that you plan out every potential risk that might arise before you invest. That quality is exactly what I'm looking for in my potential investors. Would you consider sharing your expertise as well as making x investment in my product?*

THE ASK as you see in this example is nothing more than *two sentences and a question*. We will explore this further in

Chapter 4, "How to Be an Exceptional Asker," but I wanted to introduce the idea to you now so you see how this all works *before* you ask.

If you are asking for something in your everyday life that is important to you, it is equally important that you know what money means to the person you want to ask. Suppose that you are at the doctor's office, and she has just prescribed a medication. Perhaps you do not have a prescription plan, or you want to know if there is a generic drug that is just as effective but at a lower cost. The issue is that you do not know whether your doctor will let you know of an alternative, or whether she really likes the pharmaceutical representative for this medication and will stay loyal to that person. The doctor may be loyal to the representative because he keeps her well informed and up to date on the most cutting-edge drugs. This may not appear to be a money issue, but from the doctor's viewpoint, time and education are money. You might ask,

> *I know many doctors and medical practices have pharmaceutical representatives to help them with the latest drugs for their patients; I'm sure that helps them stay current and saves them time. While I respect this process, I'm in a situation where I need to rely on generic drugs. For the medication you prescribed, is there a generic brand that is just as safe and effective, and are you willing to prescribe it for me?*

In this example, the conversation is about money. The doctor may have very strong feelings that cheaper generic drugs are not on the same level as high-end and more costly drugs, and therefore can't and won't prescribe a generic brand. Many people do not view these types of day-to-day encounters and situations as asks that involve money, but now you know and have read that they all involve money. This two-step process will make it much easier for you to ask for what you want because you are solid in your views on money and the person you are about to ask. Here's a quick review:

1. Know your views on money.
2. Know the views on money of the person you are about to ask.

Do You Have Money Wellness?

Now that you are aware of this two-step process—namely, that money is opportunity and that it is important to know your views on money and the other person's views on money before you ask—I want to drive home why I began this book, making sure you have a great relationship with money. In my e-book, *Money Wellness: Is Money Making You $ick?* (Balboa Press, 2016), I detail through numerous examples how worrying about money can lead to dreadful illnesses. It was an eye-opening experience for me, because in the course of my several careers, I experienced how money worries could cripple, devastate, and paralyze people and families. When I was working as a civil-litigation attorney, I experienced firsthand what money can do and how it affects a person's health. One of my cases involved placing 462 people from a closed mental-health facility into a hospital or community setting, with money, medication, and services. The stress this placed on these families was unbearable, because they all worried that their parent, child, uncle, sister, or brother would run out of money, and wondered who would take care of them.

As a philanthropic advisor, I have had the pleasure of working with people who value and treasure the importance of good health care, and they have made significant and transformational gifts to health care organizations. Their giving was exemplary because they knew their investment would save lives and they wanted to ensure there would be excellent health care services should they or anyone they love ever need them. I have heard many people say to me: "Health is the most important thing in life," "You can have all the money in the world, but if you don't have your health, you have nothing," and "I know in my heart that the stress and worry about money contributed to my illness."

Before I could make their philanthropic goals a reality, I discovered that many people had crazy definitions and relation-ships with money. It was taking a toll on their personal and professional lives *and on their health*. Many people could not sleep because their jobs were not paying them enough. Others were in denial that money was important or avoided seeing the doctor or having surgery to "save money." Some people took on their children's and grandchildren's debt while postponing their retirement; fell into bad eating habits, dining out all the time because work was overwhelming; avoided exercising because gyms were too expensive; or gave up their vacation and personal time because if they worked harder they would be promoted faster.

If you have any doubt that money and health are related, look up the *Stress in America Report* by the American Psychological Association. This report found that *money* was the leading source of stress.

Polls published by the Associated Press and AOL compared the physical health of people who live highly debt-stressed lives with those who live with less debt-stressed lives and found the following[1]:

- **Headaches and migraines:** 44 percent versus 15 percent
- **Depression:** 23 percent versus 4 percent
- **Heart attacks:** 6 percent versus 3 percent
- **Muscle tension and lower-back pain:** 51 percent versus 31 percent
- **Ulcers and digestive problems:** 27 percent versus 8 percent

Money is a health issue, and this stress manifests itself in our bodies and makes us ill in so many ways. Stress has been linked to many ailments, including anxiety, depression, diabetes, hair loss, obesity, obsessive-compulsive disorder, and ulcers. Many of us are stressing over saving for retirement or paying off credit card bills or school loans. Our health is suffering because we are worrying about money.

Many people think that *money wellness* means having a lot of money and being able to do anything at any time, worry free. Money wellness, however, is defined by health, not wealth. It is the sum of everything that goes with being financially, emotionally, and physically sound and is the balanced holistic integration of financial, emotional, and physical health. The thoughts, beliefs, and attitudes you have about money as well as the everyday

---

[1] *Source:* http://hosted.ap.org/specials/interactives/wdc/debt_stress/index.html

decisions you make about money affect your sleep, diet, and exercise. In fact, they affect every aspect of your life, including relationships, travel, education, parenting, fashion, real estate, charity, financial security, retirement, fun, success, and creativity. To have money wellness means having adequate cash flow, sufficient assets, the absence of illness, and the presence of emotional well-being.

Money Blockers

So how do you achieve money wellness and move beyond or avoid the physical repercussions that will come about if you worry about money? The answer is to know, address, and work through your *money blockers*. Money blockers are those little conversations we have in our heads that convince ourselves *it's not so bad* or *I'll get to this later*.

Here are some common examples of money blockers:

- I will have more savings someday.
- I am working extra hours and doing more work, so I am likely to get a nice raise or promotion.
- I don't need to ask for a raise or a promotion, because my boss will do the right thing.
- I am going to inherit my parents' house and their investments. Combined with my income, I should be set for later years.
- I pay high premiums for my insurance, so I am covered for my health, home, and business.
- Someday, I will go to those informational meetings that may or may not get me more business.
- One day, I will have that house.
- When I'm older, I can be more careful and cautious with spending. For now, I need to enjoy myself a little.
- When I'm older, I will put away more cash.
- My health insurance deductibles are high, so I should probably see a doctor only when absolutely necessary.

- I am healthy and young; I will get routine checkups later.
- I am not sleeping, because I work so much I don't have time to go to the gym, take a yoga class, or meditate.
- Later in the year, we can pay off our credit cards and get the balance to zero.
- We have to buy presents for everyone during the holidays because they buy them for us.
- We spent more than we wanted during our vacation, but we have the rest of the year to pay for it.
- When I'm in my 50s or 60s, I will focus on when to retire. For now I just have to keep a steady job and save a little.
- My children will make more money than we ever did. I am not worried about them.
- Someday, I will hit the lottery!

Do any of these sound remotely familiar? They are the scripts or scenarios we play over and over again in our heads. They put us in a coma-like state and block us from tackling our underlying concerns and worries about money. I do have suggestions for you on how you can tackle your money blockers. My first suggestion for you is to *write down your money blockers*; this is no small step to take. You will probably catch yourself in a conversation saying the same things over and over. This first step is to become aware of the expressions and stories that have carried you through to this point.

I would not ask you to do something if I did not do it myself. My money blocker for years was that I started my 403(b) when I was working at both universities; then when I transitioned into my own consulting business I never looked at the account, even in the recession years. I convinced myself that it was "safe" and that I "didn't need it now" so why should I bother moving things around in my financial portfolio? I convinced myself that as long as I periodically checked that account, all would be well. That was truly the head-in-the-sand story—out of sight, out of mind. But the truth was that I didn't have the time or the expertise to give it a thorough periodic review. Remember, time is money! So I finally hired a fabulous financial advisor who now does this for me. I could not believe I waited six years to have someone give me advice on what I should do with my 403(b). Even worse, I found out from my advisor that my self-employment fund, which I had set up in 2008, was in a cash fund, earning hardly anything. Had that been invested differently, I might have earned a lot more than I did.

Once you write all your money blockers down, I am certain you will feel much better that you acted, took control, and now have choices about what you want to do. The second step is *to substitute the familiar expressions.* For example, if you say to yourself, "I will pay my vacation credit card bills off by September," then say to yourself, "I will pay off my vacation bills right now by making a $100 payment each month." This simple mind-shift will push away your money blockers, and the more you use your new words and phrases, the better you will be at working out your money worries. Third, *be aware of other people's money blockers.* Just sit back and listen to your friends' conversations, as well as what family members say about money. You may be surprised that money worries have bonded you over the years; as the expression goes, "Misery loves company."

Now that you have developed this awareness, you may not feel as comfortable or as agreeable with other people's attitudes about money. If it comes from one of your elderly relatives, a parent, or an older sibling, you may discover that you learned to use the same negative or money-avoiding expressions because that is what the family has been saying for years. You may have heard statements like, "I don't know how we will make ends meet;" "Don't worry; it will all wash out in the end;" "Better to live well then to die poor;" "I worked all my life and, see, the government took it all way;" "I don't know what you are going to do;" "There will be no Social Security by the time you retire." Lovely thoughts aren't they? But you have the power to change all that now, because I am certain you don't want negative, repetitive phrases to shape how you feel and behave when it comes to money.

Find out which money blockers you are harboring. Work through them, and feel a sense of relief. It is far better to know that you are silently worrying about money and then do something about it than to ignore the issue. You may convince yourself that you are just fine and then find yourself with excruciating migraines or never-ending back pain. Money worries do not magically disappear on their own or over time. They can and most likely will affect your health and your spirit.

I now end this chapter on setting your course to be money well. You see, we have come full circle. We started with "What Does Money Mean to You?" and "What Does Money Mean to the Person You Are About to Ask?" We ended with how you can be and stay money well. Get straight with your views on money, know what it means to the person you are about to ask, and remove your money blockers. Money will no longer prevent you from making THE ASK.

Why Should People Ask?

I COULD ANSWER THE QUESTION IN THE chapter title in one sentence and move on to the next chapter, but you deserve much more. My one sentence is that the number-one reason why people do not get what they want is that they have not asked. Looking at this from another perspective, the number-one reason why people do not give or take action is they have not been asked. This has been tested and tested, and it's true. Human nature steers us into the false notion that if we spend time with someone; explain at length and with great detail what we want; show them charts, graphs, reports, and testimonials; and they smile while we are doing all this activity, then there is no need to ask. That person will naturally volunteer to give or to sign themselves up for the activity you just described. Spending time is not the same as making an ask.

While consulting with an organization that could not move its board to help raise funds, a board member shared with me that his style was to spend time with people, take them for coffee or lunch, meet them at the gym or networking meetings, and just "let the person do what they want to do on their own time." After all, he continued, people know why you are spending time with them, so there is no reason to pressure them to make an investment." In his words, "They will do the right thing." So I asked him over the past year exactly how much money did he raise for the organization? He never answered me directly, because the answer presumably was very little or even zero. So I asked him to shift his thinking for a bit. I told him that I had spent a lot of time with donors and investors and, when not asked directly, they *assume* their money is not needed. They *assume* you have plenty of other donors or investors and their money, time, or expertise is not important.

Spending all this time and attention without making an ask sends the wrong signal. You do need to get to know people before you ask. You need to find out if they are interested in what you do and are willing to learn more. But at some point you will need to ask; otherwise, why begin these engagement activities at all? The vast majority of people will not give unless they are asked. If they do give without being asked, I guarantee you the amount will be far less than what you wanted, and their time and activity with you will be far less than what you expected.

Top 10 Reasons Why You Should Ask

Now that you know you need to make the ask so that nothing is left to chance, here are my top 10 reasons why you should ask.

1. ASKING IS EMPOWERING ON EVERY LEVEL. This is my overall favorite reason for why you should ask. When you ask, you are expressing and showing to the world that you have a plan, you have a course of action, you thought long and hard about what you want, and *you deserve it*. That last point, that you deserve it, is what I believe prevents most people from asking. I receive many calls and requests to help people get out of their miserable jobs. Think right now how many friends, relatives, neighbors, colleagues, acquaintances, and people you meet at networking meetings, conferences, and seminars simply hate what they do or feel stuck in their jobs? I'm guessing you could count at least 10 or more. Why would anyone spend upwards of 75 percent of their life doing something that does not fulfill them or give them a purpose in life?

It's not the money that keeps them stuck in their jobs. *What keeps them stuck in their misery is that they haven't asked.* You can ask for a raise, a new job title, a job relocation, a promotion, more paid time off, more vacation time, time off to volunteer, a sabbatical, or more money for training, conferences, seminars, webinars, or formal education, and you don't always have to leave your place of employment to get all those wonderful perks. It begins with your asking.

I was happily working at one university when another university asked me to consider moving to another city for its top fundraising job and to head a $100 million capital campaign. I thought to myself that having the top-line staff position and reporting to the university president would be fantastic. While this was a tremendous opportunity, I knew nothing about the university. It would be a big risk and a big move. Instead of turning it down right away because it would take time to interview and moving is never fun, I called everyone I knew in fundraising and asked them they knew about the university, was it a good place to work, what was its fundraising reputation, did its board help with fundraising, what did they know about the president, and were there any alumni I should call? Asking for information is a great ask because you can't make an important decision until you have the information you need. For me, I felt great and *empowered* because I asked the right questions to make one of the most important decisions in my career. Three months later, I took the job, and I've been living blissfully in New York City—the West Village I might add—ever since.

If you don't ask, you will feel worse, stuck like some friends, family, and colleagues who commiserate with you about their unhappiness. Turn this around, and take one small step toward what you want. This will empower you and give you all the confidence in the world that you are in charge of your life, your happiness, and your destiny, and that you can and will make the right decision. Indecision is agony. It is draining and stressful, leads to sleepless nights, and can bring on all sorts of illnesses. Visualize that when you ask, you are in your power suit, like an action figure or some person that you most admire. Put the power suit on, ask, and be empowered.

2. ASKING LEADS TO MONEY AND SUCCESS. Who does not want money and success? Remember the number-one reason why people do not give is that they have not been asked. You cannot expect people to be mind readers. The very definition of mind reading says it all. Mind reading is the seemingly magical ability to map someone's mental terrain from their words, emotions, and body language. I love the emphasis on "magical ability." Do you really

want to place someone in the position of reading your mind to know what exactly it is that you want? That seems to me a big burden to place on anyone even if they had the capability. But that is exactly what you do when you do not make a specific ask. I have said this and will continue to emphasize it throughout the book: *Don't leave it to chance.* That is what you do when you don't ask. You will have far more money for your passion project and be off-the-charts successful in any venture when you ask.

3. ASKING ATTRACTS LIKE-MINDED PEOPLE TO YOU, YOUR PASSION, AND YOUR LIFE. We all want to be around like-minded people so that we can all enjoy, learn, and grow with each other. Think back when someone asked you to volunteer, help, lend a hand, take over a responsibility, be on a board, mentor, sponsor, present, create a new product, carve out a different approach, make a recommendation, serve as a reference, have your child make a play date with another child, or join a team. If you said yes, you probably did so to be around them and enjoy their company as well as for the experience.

4. ASKING CREATES PERSONAL MOMENTUM, ENTHUSIASM, AND ENERGY. I love the words "personal momentum." It's one thing to have momentum, which is movement and action. It's another when it's personal momentum, because now it's internalized. It's all about your personal goals and growth. When you ask, it creates forward motion because you are putting yourself out there. When you ask, it creates energy and enthusiasm because you are asking for something that is meaningful and important to you. One of my favorite expressions is "Be that forward-moving train, and ask for what you want."

5. ASKING BOOSTS SELF-WORTH FOR VITAL EVERYDAY NEEDS. Personal momentum and self-worth go hand in hand. This is particularly true in personal relationships. For example, let's say there is a couple who have been going out for a few years and they decide it's time to move in together. They are excited to select the apartment in the right location. They move in, and things start going downhill. She works long hours and travels a great deal, while

he is left to do the basics, shop, cook, clean, walk the dog, and arrange their social time. He starts getting resentful but does not speak up. Soon he is not sleeping well, he gets distracted at work, and his friends are getting tired of his complaining about how she does not pull her weight. In essence, his self-worth is tanking. A lot of this can be avoided and resolved by making simple and sincere asks. He can say "I know and appreciate that your work is demanding and that your travel is brutal. There are many things to do when you are not home, and I'm sure we both want more of a balance between work and having a great home life. Can we talk about the ways we can divide up these responsibilities?" Remember, *the ask is two sentences and a question.* When you ask, you feel empowered and in control and your self-worth and self-esteem are elevated.

6. ASKING INVITES POSITIVE AND POWERFUL OUTCOMES. When you think about it, an ask is an invitation—an invitation to do something, such as help a friend, join a prayer group, get more information, seek financial advice, share expertise, hold a door open, support a local charity, make an investment, create a solution, or fix a software problem. These are everyday occurrences, yet we don't think about them in terms of an ask; we think of them in terms of things we need to get done. The next time you need to get something done and ask for help, take a minute to see how you feel. I guarantee you will feel pretty good because you are about to resolve an issue or celebrate an accomplishment.

Your ask is an invitation, and invitations have a positive and upbeat connotation both for the person asking as well as the person who needs help. People are flattered that you asked them. Test this: How do you feel when someone asks you for help? Even if you can't help them, you feel good that they asked you. My favorite illustration is someone on the street or highway asking for directions. People love to share their knowledge and experience to guide a person to their destination. Watch them. They make deliberate pointing motions on the map, their hands are waving in the air in the direction they need to take, and they stand there to make sure the person sets off in the right direction. The person needing directions no longer feels lost and unsure. How powerful and rewarding is that feeling? The ask invites these types of positive and powerful outcomes for both the person asking and the person being asked.

7. ASKING STOPS THE SECOND-GUESSING BY TAKING ACTION. I was speaking at a women's conference at the United Nations and agreed to raffle off a free half-hour session on THE ASK. The conference organizer wanted me to give the winner an hour, but I said no. I wanted the person who won this to know that whenever you ask for advice, you need to organize your thoughts so that you maximize the person's time. Half an hour will show that you had all your questions and asks lined up and ready to go. The woman who won the raffle was thrilled. She was young and very bright and lived in Chicago. At the conference we arranged our half-hour call. One week later she called me. She was a great listener because she had her "script" ready to go. She had started a business creating a nursing blouse for women who needed to breastfeed and told me of her revenue projections over the next three years. Earlier she had shared with me that she had a master's degree in business administration, so I was not surprised that she was in her comfort zone working with numbers.

I stopped her about four minutes into our conversation and asked her, "Where will your first $75,000 in start-up costs come from?" She hesitated at first then said she planned on asking her family. I asked her which family member and how much was she planning to ask each one. She said she wasn't sure but was counting on them to get the $75,000. She thought she could ask her brother for $25,000 first, but then again her uncle had more money, so maybe she should ask him first. Her sister-in-law was doing well with her business so maybe she should start with her. She told me she wanted to win the session with me so that I could tell her who she should ask for which amount and in what order.

This is a classic example of second-guessing. Our bright young entrepreneur had been mulling over these asks for months while designing her blouse and thinking that her family might or might not cover the $75,000 start-up costs. She shared with me that she thought if they saw the new product and saw how busy and dedicated she was to the new business that they would offer to invest with her.

So I put a dead end to the "ask guess game" as I call it, and we worked out her family asks and the exact language she could use. As it turned out, she needed to ask only one family member and then she had her start-up money. Asking ends the unnecessary guessing of what the person you want to ask might do. It also is a much better use of your time so that you can get back to your creative projects.

8. ASKING TURNS THE UNEXPECTED INTO LEVERAGED OPPORTUNITY. My budding nursing-blouse entrepreneur circled back with me a few months later. She now needed to find people beyond her family that she could ask for funding. We came up with a short list of her colleagues that she could ask. I told her to pick a colleague from our list and practice her ask with me. She started out sounding so clinical and business-like that I stopped her and asked "You know this person pretty well don't you?" She said yes; they went to business school together and were good friends. So I told her *share your why in your ask.* She had no idea what I was talking about so I asked her, "Why did you start this business in the first place?" And there it was—her why. She was working for a large company and doing a lot of travel on planes. After the birth of her first child, while still traveling, she had no privacy on a plane to nurse her child. All the delicate blankets kept falling off, embarrassing her and her plane seatmates. She decided to create a stylish blouse that could open up easily for the mother so the baby could nurse and all would be covered to avoid embarrassment. I told her that was brilliant and that she needed to share this simple story and then do her ask.

Not only did she receive additional investments from her colleagues, she also received names of people who might be interested in investing in her company as well as referrals to major company buyers who might want to have her product in their stores. The ask is so much more than getting what you want in the present; it gives you *leveraged opportunities for the future.*

9. ASKING MAKES TOUGH-TO-DISCUSS ISSUES DOABLE. I know I'll have a hard time convincing you of this reason to ask! As you will read in Chapter 3, tackling tough issues is a reason why many people do not ask. After all it may be easier to avoid a tough issue than to address it with an ask, even if the ask is as gentle as "Can we talk about what is bothering you?"

As we saw in Chapter 1, money is embedded in every decision you will make, so it is natural that most tough-to-discuss issues involve money. Now that you know the importance of knowing what money means to you, how to remove your money blockers, and the questions you need to ask to find out what money means to the person you want to ask for money, suddenly the tough-to-discuss issues should not seem so tough or insurmountable. Let's take for example the need for you to cut back on your spending. Perhaps you have some outstanding credit card debt, loan, or medical bill or you need to save for college, a new car, a major repair, or retirement. Your family still wants the elaborate holiday gift exchange, your best friend wants her destination wedding, or your significant other wants to spend now and save later. These are all tough-to-discuss issues because you don't want to take away the other person's joy or good time, but you also do not want to cave in and spend more now because you need to save.

Asking to the rescue! Think of asking as your personal Mighty Mouse, the superhero cartoon mouse whose theme song had the refrain, "Here I come to save the day!" The tough-to-discuss issue is that you do not want to seem tight with your money or that you are in such a financial bind that you can't spend what others expect you to spend. Asking can lessen your stress by saying,

I know it is important to the family that we show our love for each other with thoughtful and wonderful gifts this holiday. This year I need to conserve my spending because my goal is to wipe out all my credit card debt. Do you think we could just give the kids gifts this year and have the adults just appreciate each other's time?

I couldn't be happier for you and having your wedding in Anguilla, and what an honor it is to be invited. This is very difficult to say, but I'm still paying off a major and unexpected medical bill and I'm halfway there.

Can we talk about how I can still be part of your wedding without participating in all the activities?

I know how much we both like going away each year to visit our friends in Italy. At the same time we are saving for our vacation home, which may wind up to be our retirement home. Can we talk about the possibility of postponing the trip and explaining to them that we love them but we do need to conserve our resources this year?

THE ASK—it's two sentences and a question. Have I convinced you that it makes the tough-to-discuss issues just a little bit easier?

10. ASKING ENHANCES YOUR STATUS AMONG YOUR PEERS. Here are some scenarios that may sound familiar to you: "I recruited three colleagues to serve on our committee," "I got my neighbor to volunteer for our fair," "We went to the boss and now we have dress-down Fridays," "The rabbi found us a new director for our youth camp," or "I landed an enormous new account for the company." What do they all have in common? In addition to having positive and successful outcomes, all of these scenarios involved asks. You can't get new committee members, volunteers, a dress-down day at work, a new youth-camp director, or a new account unless you ask for them. That is part one. Part two is that you had a sense of admiration, a strong positive feeling about the person who shared their success—their successful ask. This is precisely why I say when you ask, it enhances your status amongst your peers. They think so highly of you because you are getting what you want because you put yourself out there and asked. It's human nature to want people to think well of you, and when you ask they do.

Even if you do not get what you asked for, people will still think highly of you. For example, when you hear "I asked her, and she turned us down," "I did my best, but he said no," or "They are really not ready to decide. This may take us longer," I think you would agree that you still look up to the speaker for making the ask. Asking, regardless of the answer, does enhance how your peers think of you. Now you have more than enough reasons why it is important to ask.

WHEN NOT TO ASK

Let's take the reverse position (this is an occupational hazard of mine, as a lawyer). Is there ever a time when you should *not* ask? The answer is "Yes, in my experience there are times when you should not ask." The first instance is when it would be insensitive to ask.

The Person You Want to Ask Is Going Through a Rough Time

I had a visit scheduled with a couple who wanted to make a very large gift to an organization where I was working. We had been discussing exactly what they wanted to do, but we had not solidified the exact amount. They needed time to meet with their financial planner and to work out some details with their other philanthropic priorities. When I arrived at their home, only the wife was there, and I assumed the husband would be arriving any minute. We began making some small talk about the summer and the weather, but I noticed she was a bit distracted. Then the telephone rang, and her face looked very distraught. She hung up the telephone and continued our conversation. Something still was not right. I said to her that I had wanted to talk with her and her husband about some ideas I had in mind for their prospective gift, but it was not the right time. I let her know that I sensed she was dealing with something very important and troubling and that we could do this another time. She looked relieved and hugged me as I left, and I told her that our organization was there for whatever we could do to help her with her situation.

Now this may be an obvious case of bad timing, but I do know some people who would have asked for the large gift, specifying the amount and purpose just to get it out and then leave. Some people have the anxiety rush to ask, and then they feel their job is done. How insensitive would it have been if I had asked her right in her moment of distress? The point is to gauge the level of how *present* the person is when you are about to make your ask. If they seem distracted, aloof, unfocused, or preoccupied, your ask will get lost and will be meaningless. I believe it is always best to say you *wanted* to share with them an opportunity or *wanted* to ask them for feedback or help, but it can wait; they come first.

You Are Not Ready or You Are Unsure of Your Ask

The second instance of when you should not ask is when you are *unsure of your ask*. Let's say during a staff meeting your boss revealed that the company is opening up a new branch and that it would be determining who should lead this upcoming project. This assignment would be perfect for you because you would love to relocate and gain additional managerial responsibilities. You make an appointment to see your boss to ask her if you can be chosen to lead this new project. Your boss asks you why you want the assignment, what three things you will do to make this branch the most profitable in the company, what strategic and critical skills you will share with your new employees, and what partnerships you will form in this new community. You had not prepared for any of these questions, so to ask for the job now would be fruitless. As you will read in Chapter 4, "How to Be an Exceptional Asker," without preparation, there can be no ask. This illustration highlights the importance of preparing inside and out before you ask. This situation could be saved by stating that the boss's questions were excellent and that you would come back in a few days with answers to those questions and any others she may have, and then you would ask for the job.

Your Ask Will Be Confusing

The third instance of when you should not ask is when you will be *confusing the person* you are about to ask to the point where they could not possibly make a decision. This happens often when two people are doing the ask. For example, let's say you are a board member and you want to bring a fellow board member with you to ask a colleague to join the board. You sit down with your prospective board member, and you explain the rules and responsibilities (i.e., that all board members need to attend quarterly meetings, they must be assigned to a committee, they must attend special events, and they are expected to make a meaningful annual gift). Your co-asker jumps in and says that while they do want everyone to give each year, not everyone does, and some attend events and some do not. Your prospective board member then has a quizzical look and asks whether she has to give each year and states quite frankly that special events are not her thing, so if she joins the board can she skip the events? Both board members look at each other and say they really don't know, but don't worry something can be worked out. How much a person is obligated to give each year and what the expectations are in terms of participation are very critical pieces of information any board member needs to know before making a major commitment to a board. This illustrates how confusing conversations and unclear facts can muddle well-intended asks. I am by no means suggesting that you need to know every fact and figure before you ask, but you do need to know the important elements of your ask. In this case, the board members should have had a clear and consistent idea of what the roles and responsibilities were for becoming a board member before they ask someone to be a board member. If the person being asked wanted to know some things in addition to the roles and responsibilities involved, that's fine; in fact, it could add to a meaningful conversation.

The bottom line is that if your ask will confuse the person being asked or contradict previous conversations, you must get your facts lined up before you ask. Otherwise you will be spending a lot of time during the ask sorting out the confusion, which really will dilute the impact and power of your ask.

ASKING MANTRAS THAT WILL SERVE YOU WELL

I wanted to end this chapter with my favorite asking mantras. A mantra is a word or phrase that is repeated often or that expresses someone's basic beliefs. I created these asking mantras because they have helped me to stay focused on why it is so important to ask the right way. They also have helped the people I work with push away their fears about asking. They create a mindset of nothing but positive energy to get positive results. Many times when I am training boards or sales teams or simply speaking with someone who wants to ask a friend for money but feels it is an imposition, I use these asking mantras because it puts the world of asking into perspective. I print them out on a large piece of paper, laminate them, and give them to the people who have a hard time asking. They can serve as a reminder of some the most important aspects about asking. So here are my asking mantras.

*The Quality of Your Life Is Determined by the Quality
Questions You Ask Yourself and Others*

I must say this is one of my more recent asking mantras, and I just
love it! Think about it; questions are so powerful and quality
questions are electrifying. Quality questions bring you closer to the
person you want to engage. They say to the person, "You are
important and meaningful to me and I want to know you better."
Quality questions I like to ask people are:

*What is the first memory you had when you knew it was important to
give back?*

*When and if we form this partnership, how do we fulfill each other's
expectations?*

What does money mean to you? (You knew I would ask that one from
Chapter 1.)

*If and when you were to do something transformational with us, what
would that look like?*

When you give us money, where do you think it goes?

What would it take for you to say yes?

Where are we on your top philanthropic priorities?

This is truly so important to us; is it as important to you?

These quality questions invite people to reflect on what is
important to them, and it gets very quickly to the heart of the
matter—your ask. They enable you to learn so much more about
the person that it's like having a window into their soul. You could
ask dry and factual questions in a business setting, but it's so much
more enriching when you connect personally and build trust and
loyalty with your boss, clients, co-workers, family, and friends.
That is why you ask quality questions.

The second part of this asking mantra is the questions you ask
yourself. Do you challenge yourself enough by asking yourself the
right questions? In order to be an extraordinary asker (as you will

read in Chapter 4), you have to be prepared to ask yourself the right quality questions:

Am I a good listener?

Do I believe 100 percent in my ask?

Am I giving this person my undivided attention?

Am I present in all my asks?

Am I persistent, not pushy, when I ask?

What did I learn from this experience and how can I use it going forward?

Who can help me navigate this situation?

Do my sincerity and energy shine through when I ask?

I have so many more that I use, but this should give you an idea of the quality questions you can and should ask yourself every day. Here is an example of how this can increase your success, which in turn increases your quality of life. A major food retailer was looking for a consultant to help them form a charitable foundation. They invited me to apply to be their consultant. Before the interview, I asked myself many questions, such as "Why do I want this job?" "Why should they hire me?" What distinguishes me from the pack?" and "What if they make enormous demands that I know I can't deliver?" During the interview they asked me what would be my fee. I share with them that I work on a retainer basis and gave them my retainer fee. One person on the search committee asked me why I thought I was worth my monthly retainer? It was a variation of the question I had prepared to answer but in much less gracious terms. So I thought to myself, "Do they really know who they are asking this question of—an attorney and the expert on the ask?" As you can see, I have a healthy ego, but I thought this question was in really bad taste. I contained myself and thought for a few seconds about my response. To my surprise I turned it around and asked him if he had researched or Googled me prior to the interview? He said he had. Then I said to him, "You already have your answer. You should hire me and at my retainer fee because I am the best and your work requires the best." Four days later, I got the consulting job. I asked myself the right questions, which mentally prepared me to deliver that answer confidently, not obnoxiously or seemingly unprepared.

Focusing on these questions has put my asking skills on a whole different level, which is why I say it determines your quality of life. It greatly enhanced mine, and I'm counting on it to enhance yours.

When You Ask for Money, You Are Not Taking Something Away; You Are Giving an Opportunity

This asking mantra gets my second vote. I've used this one for over two decades, and it's the one that make people stop and at least give asking for money a try. Many people have told me that when they ask for money they visualize it leaving people's pockets, wallets, bank accounts, and retirement accounts and taking precious resources away from their family, travel, enjoyment, faith, creativity, recreation, health, and education.

Many people have the hardest time asking the people who are closest to them for money. You may want to ask a neighbor to buy a book of raffle tickets for your block association, a co-worker to sponsor you in a race, a colleague to buy a table for your gala, friends to give to your crowdfunding website, or a relative to invest in your business. All of these asks get blanketed with your emotional connection to the person you want to ask. You start to do what I call "fill-in-the-blank fundraising" and leap to assumptions before you even ask. You assume the person will feel awkward and uncomfortable, not want to do it, turn around and ask you for something, or, worse yet, put distance in your relationship. You make all these assumptions, and you haven't even given the person the opportunity to hear what you have to say.

Whenever I hear someone say they can't ask a close friend, relative, neighbor, or colleague for money I change their minds by sharing the following. When you *don't* ask the people who are closest to you, they think there is a circle of people richer, smarter, better, and more important to you than they are and they are not in that circle. Take a deep breath and re-read that sentence because it is true. I have asked many people who *were not asked* how they felt when someone they knew very well needed to raise money for either an important cause or a personal project and they were not asked to help out. They felt left out and not important. The worst part is that it makes them feel that they are not rich enough to be asked.

How you ask the people who are closest to you is the key to including them and giving them the *opportunity* to invest in your cause or in you. Here is how I ask people for money who are close to me, and it has worked successfully for the people who use this approach:

> *Marty, you know I am on the board of the theater and have been for over eight years. We are celebrating our 50th anniversary with a spectacular retrospect of our top productions on October 15. I have no idea if you are interested in supporting this anniversary celebration but can we have a conversation and talk about it?*

THE ASK—it's two sentences and a question.

I select my words very carefully. I lay out what my role is within the organization and why this is important to me and then invite my closest people to join me in the conversation about their possible support. It's one of my favorite asks. Trust me; I learned this from all my mistakes. I am on several boards, and I do a lot of fundraising for them. When I share these fundraising events with my friends and family *after they have happened,* most of them say to me they would have loved to come or would have loved to have supported it *if they had known.* What they are really saying is "Why didn't you share this with me before? I would have participated." What they are really saying is *why didn't you ask me?* Clearly, I missed the moment to present the opportunity to my friends and family.

Here is another example you can use:

> *Brittany, while we have been friends since high school and this may seem awkward, I didn't want to exclude you from sharing my excitement about my new virtual-reality sunglasses. We are at the point where we are seeking some strategic investor partners, and I thought of you. I would love to have you involved so can we talk a bit about it and see if you have any interest in investing in our new product?*

Again my words are carefully chosen. I get out right away that it may be "awkward" and that I didn't want to "exclude" her. I share with Brittany that the timing is right and that I'm at the point where we need investment partners. If I hadn't selected these words, she might assume I've asked a million people and she was the last one. I use the words "strategic investor partners" because that lets her know it's not just the money we are seeking, it's also her critical and strategic thinking. My ask is an invitation and an opportunity to invest.

THE ASK is an opportunity. It takes nothing away and is filled only with possibilities.

THE ASK Is a Conversation, Not a Confrontation

I have experienced plenty of asks over my career, and the ones that bother me the most are the ones that come across as confrontational. No one ever intends to do that, but it is either the asker's nervousness or overly zealous nature that makes it sound and feel harsh. Here are some examples of what I mean:

> Bill, you just have to do it. You know and I know it's the right thing, so that's a yes?

> Sarah, I don't need to repeat myself, but you will say yes, right?

> Kyle, if you can't do it, we have to close up shop, and you would not want that, would you?

> Jennifer, your business partners are in so I don't really have to ask you, do I?"

These examples are not exactly the rapport-building, harmonious relationship building we were looking for during the ask. These may be well-intended asks, but they come off as harsh. I've asked people afterwards who have been asked this way to describe how they felt, and they generally compare it to a tennis match. I speak, you speak, I speak, you speak, back and forth, back and forth. By the end of three rounds of this type of talk the person being asked is completely clueless as to what the person is asking.

So I want you to think of every ask as a conversation. It is circular and inviting. The ask should have a warm tone. It should *contain a bit of information* you know about the person or their interest, which is *directly tied to your ask*. For example (and this is an easy one), if you know the person loves to play golf and you are running a charity golf tournament you could say, "I know how much you love golf, and I'm sure your game is much better than mine. I'm helping the club to run a benefit golf tournament that supports children with cancer, and I think you would really enjoy yourself and meet some new business contacts. It's the second Friday in May—might you be interested in playing for a great cause?" Think of what could have been asked using this same example: "It's golf time and I've got just the tournament for you. At the club we have a spectacular day lined up and it has your name all over it. Are you in?" That approach can work for some but when it comes to asking for money, the lighter and more personal touch always wins the day. Even if you know someone inside out, they do like to be asked in a conversational way that gives them the opportunity to ask questions and to make thoughtful decisions.

My advice is that you become aware of the words you select and the manner in which you deliver them when you ask. No one wants to feel as if their back is against the wall, an enormous spotlight is beaming on them, and then they have to make a split-second, on-the-spot decision. Conversational tones, reinforcing the match between the person's interest and your opportunity will get you much further to yes for your ask.

Why People Do Not Ask

NOW THAT WE KNOW THE REASONS WHY everyone should ask, and there are many, let's take a look at why people don't ask. I always think it is best that we work through the things that may get in the way of making your ask. Then you will be in perfect alignment to make an exceptional ask, as we shall see in Chapter 4.

When I ask people who need to ask but are resistant to do so what gets in the way when they want to ask, they usually say "fear." At first I thought they meant fear of hearing the word "no." So I asked them to clarify what exactly they are afraid of. Many people do say it's hearing the word "no," but others say it's fear of rejection or alienating the person they are asking. So I take these emotions apart one by one, because fear, rejection, and alienation are emotions.

Let's begin with hearing the word "no." My question is: If you fear hearing "no," is that the worst word you have heard in your life? I doubt it. In reality you will hear "no" when you ask. Remember, when you ask, you are giving someone an opportunity. They may say yes to the opportunity or turn you down. The goal when you hear the word "no" is to *find out why*. Why did someone not want to do what you asked? We will go in great depth on this very issue in Chapter 6, "How to Keep Your ASK on Track." If you can get to the underlying reason, you will have a very good chance of going back to the person you asked, recognizing what was missing in your ask, and, yes, making the ask again.

Fear of rejection is common because, after all, rejection is negative, it's dismissive, and it feels like an elimination of the purpose behind your ask. You can turn this fear around by remembering one small and simple statement. When someone you are asking says no to your ask and a feeling of rejection comes up for you, the person is not rejecting *you,* they are just turning down your request. This is much easier to say than to do, I know. If you can say to yourself that it is not about you, it's about what you asked, it will remove you and keep you from feeling rejected.

THE TOP 15 REASONS WHY PEOPLE DO NOT ASK

Over the years, I made a list of reasons that people have shared with me for why they do not want to ask. Many will sound familiar to you while others may not resonate as well. I listed them in the order that I hear them the most, with number one—fear of rejection and hearing no—as the most often-cited reason why people do not ask. In addition to listing the reasons, I give you advice on how to address them so that you and any co-askers you may have can ask with confidence. Here is the list in order of priority.

1. THE FEAR OF REJECTION AND OF HEARING NO. Hopefully, you have enough tools shared in this chapter to arm you against feeling rejected or dejected and you can use this as an opportunity to ask again in the future.

2. YOU ARE NOT 100 PERCENT COMMITTED TO YOUR ASK. A local group that was organizing a 5-k run asked me to come in for the day to speak with their volunteers. There were about 30 volunteers in this session, and they were responsible for asking their friends, family, colleagues, and anyone in their network to sponsor the run at a $250, $500, or $1,000 level. Before I began, I asked them to tell me why they got involved with this group. Many said because a friend asked them to help raise money for the race. Then I asked them what they knew about this group. Many said something very vague like "They do good work" or "It's a good cause." So I asked them how strong and persuasive do they think their ask will be if they are not 100 percent committed to the mission of this organization? They looked at me with blank stares, and many looked down or looked away. My last and final question to them was "Could this be the reason why they have yet to ask their friends, their family, their colleagues, or their network?"

Whenever you ask, you should be 100 percent committed—all in, with absolute certainty that this is what you want for your organization, your business, your personal growth, and your happiness. When people sense that you are not 100 percent committed, they will very rarely say yes to your ask. I have an expression that has served me well over the years: "When you ask, people see right through you." They can tell, sense, and read whether you are or are not passionate, committed, convincing, and energetic about your ask. Please do not think you can disguise this, because you cannot. I have been with people who did their best to disguise their discomfort or their detachment with their ask, and it all fell apart. Be the one who is 100 percent committed, own your ask, and watch the response.

3. THE DREADED QUID PRO QUO, THAT YOU WILL BE ASKED FOR MONEY IN RETURN. This one is an easy one to overcome. Will you be asked for money if you ask for money? Maybe you will, or maybe you will not. When you are in that situation where someone asks you for money back, you have choices. You can either support or invest in what they are asking or not. But this should not prevent you from pre-selecting who you ask if you really want to ask a person but sense she may ask you back in return. Again, this leaping assumption that if you ask them, they will ask you (so as a result you do not ask at all) is entirely made up in your head. It is an assumption you have created. You may be leaving a lot of money on the proverbial table if you don't ask or choose to ask only the "safer" people who you sense will not ask you back.

Additionally, remember, those people who are closest to you know what you do and that you have to raise money. To leave them out of your asking possibilities distances them. Unless a friend, relative, colleague, or neighbor tells you "please do not ask me for money," you have nothing to lose and everything to gain. Revisit Chapter 2, "Asking Mantras," for examples of how you can ask with sensitivity so that you feel good about asking those people closest to you, even if you sense they may ask you in return.

4. THE AWKWARD AND UNCOMFORTABLE SITUATION THAT RESULTS FROM ASKING YOUR SPOUSE OR PARTNER FOR SOMETHING PERSONAL. I am purposely focusing on the personal ask with someone you love because this can be incredibly difficult. There is a lot at stake, because you may put distance into the relationship when you ask for something that is personal and important to you. I know many couples who struggle with getting more time for each other. Life and work get in the way of their time as a couple. If both parties are not on the same page as to how much time is the right time to spend with each other, arguments begin. Worse yet is when one person feels that he or she is spending the right amount of time with the partner and life is just fine, while the other partner is stewing and building resentment to the point of feeling abandoned and taken for granted.

What prevents the ask in personal relationships? First, we all want to have our conversations be nice and loving. When you ask for something that may surprise the other person, or if you don't know whether the other person feels the same way, that's a risk. When it's a risk, we retreat and we don't ask. Second, many times there is an expectation that, since you are so close, the person should do what you want without asking. How often have you heard the questions "Do I really have to ask for it? Shouldn't you know what to do?" The problem with expectations is that they go unspoken. In the example of our couple where one is happy and content with their shared time while the other is building resentment about the lack of shared time, the unhappy partner *expects* their special one to naturally know that they need more time and to just make it happen.

Without the ask, it does not happen and will not happen. This can all be resolved in a gentle and caring way if the unhappy partner says,

> *I miss when we do not spend the weekend and a weeknight or two just for ourselves, and I hope you do. Our time together keeps me so close to you and I feel so empty when we do not share that quality time. Can we talk about how we together can work on making that happen?*

5. YOU DON'T KNOW WHAT AMOUNT TO ASK. This can be particularly difficult to determine, and I have seen this more times than I care to in philanthropy. A new potential supporter is identified for the nonprofit. She becomes educated and involved with the

organization's mission. After she expresses great interest in helping the organization, it is time to ask her for money. Suddenly, because the development person does not have absolute certainty about what this new prospect can give, even if massive amounts of prospect research have been done previously, the development person postpones the ask. It also happens quite often when entrepreneurs need backers, investors for the business.

When you are in this situation of not knowing how much to ask for try using these words:

Emily, you graciously shared with us that your primary interest in our elementary school is that the children have field trips to cultural events in our city. We have no idea if you can make a gift of this size, but we ask you now to consider making a gift of $50,000 that will cover the costs of two field trips a year for every child in our elementary school. What do you think about this amazing opportunity?

Kyle, I've set up a crowdfunding site for my new business because I'm seeking to raise the remaining $20,000. I have no idea if you could make an investment of this size, but I would love for you to make the first gift on the site for $5,000 so that others will join you and make similar investments of this size. How does that sound to you?

In the example with Emily, it is important that if you know what the person is most interested in with your organization you reference that in your ask. That is what I call "the match." It matches the person's key interest with an opportunity for your organization or business. In the example with Kyle, it is also a good idea to let the person know that their investment *will attract others to give in similar amounts.* That is a real multiplier effect. People are often hesitant to give if they think they will be the only one giving. When you say that their investment will attract other investments, that wakes them up and suddenly they are with you in your effort to raise money.

For both of the examples above, I use the phrase "I have no idea if you can make a gift/investment of this size." If you really do not know, this is a great phrase to use because it is honest. It also keeps the ask in focus. By that I mean you are showcasing and placing the emphasis on the project or program to be funded, not the amount. During your ask, you should make sure the person is really interested in your project or program before you ask for the money to fund it. Suppose in the preceding examples I had said,

> *Emily, we really need $50,000 in order to give our elementary school children access to three field trips a year.*
>
> *Kyle, $5,000 will jumpstart my crowdfunding effort. Can you do it?*

Do you see the difference between leading and focusing on the amount and not the importance of the projects? When you place all the emphasis on the amount, the person being asked detaches and feels that they are just being asked for their money, not their involvement.

6. YOU DON'T KNOW WHO SHOULD MAKE THE ASK. Instead of focusing on who should make the ask, flip this around. With each ask, think of the person you are about to ask. The asker then needs to be someone the person knows, likes, and trusts. That's my rule. People feel really comfortable if they are asked by someone they know, like, and trust. The ask does not go well at all if a complete stranger makes it, if the person being asked does not like the asker, or the if the asker is not trustworthy. Every ask requires strategy, so when you are lining up people you would like to ask, consider each person one by one and think of who would be the best person to make the ask. If it is someone besides you or in addition to you, then make sure that person is brought into the process early. For example, if you want to bring on a new board member, committee member, or volunteer and you believe that a fellow board member should do the ask with you, then from the first meeting make sure that board member is with you.

Asks go very badly when a brand-new person is brought in to make the ask. I know this firsthand. I was working with a donor who wanted to make a very large gift to the university. I got to know this donor and his family very well over the course of seven months. We had discussed the parameters of his gift: when he could make it as well as what portion of the gift would come from his liquid assets and what portion from his will. The day arrived when he was scheduled to come to my office so that we could go over the details of his gift and he could sign the gift agreement.

A person in a leadership role at the university who knew the donor only slightly called me one hour before my meeting and said that he had called the donor. The donor was coming to his office, so I should deliver the gift agreement to his office but not be part of the meeting. At first I thought this would be great since it is always impressive when a person in a leadership position is involved in high-end asks. Then I got this very uneasy feeling because I did not know what the relationship was between these two men. I asked if I could be part of the meeting, just to listen and to do any follow-up that was needed. The answer was no. (That is an ask right there—asking to be part of an important meeting.)

The meeting took place without me. About one hour after the meeting I received a telephone call from the donor. He was irate, upset, and angry. He told me the university would never receive a dime from him. To this day, I have no idea what happened. Could I have changed the results if I had been in the room? I may never know. The one thing I did learn and I do know now is that it is really important to apply the *know, like, and trust,* rule when selecting the asker.

7. YOU DON'T KNOW WHEN TO ASK. I often say if I had a quarter for every time a person asked me "How do I know the person is ready to be asked?" I would own Manhattan! I have an expression and it really applies here: People leave clues; we miss every one of them.

Take this scenario: You are explaining and outlining your project or something you need with a friend. Your friend turns to you and says, "What do you need to make this happen?" "What do you need from me?" or "How can I help you?" Nine times out of ten you keep explaining your need and skip right over this clue. The clue is that they are *asking you to ask them* for what you want. If you want money, this is the time to ask for it. If you want help, this is the time to ask for it. If you want advice or a referral, this is the time to ask for it. So become that superior listener, and the time to ask will become obvious.

What if you do not receive these questions and you are still unsure. I have two more tips for you. First, let your instincts be your guide. If you *feel* the person is ready to be asked, do it. This is what we call the gut test. There is not a whole lot to explain because it is something you have to feel. This requires you to be really focused and present in your conversations and interactions with the person you will eventually ask.

Second, whenever I am stuck and really do not know, I create structure. Years ago I created "Laura's readiness formula." I have used this as a guide to judge whether a person is ready to be asked so here we go:

$$Education + Involvement + Inclination + Assets = The\ Right\ Time$$

A person needs to be educated and to have a certain level of knowledge about your ask. Think about yourself. Would you willingly do something if you did not know anything about it? Probably not. Next, the person needs to be a bit involved. This naturally varies from person to person, but my rule is that the larger the ask, the more involvement is needed. If you need a relative to take care of your children while you are having surgery and recovering for a few months, that relative really needs to be involved. He will need to know your children's schedules, what they eat, when they sleep, what after-school activities they do, what they like to do in their free time, and how many hours they are allowed on their smartphones and video games.

The hardest part of this formula is *inclination*. Visualize a playground with a seesaw that right now is perfectly level. If you think the person is inclined to be asked and your instincts say the person is inclined, then you need to ask and the seesaw goes up. If you think the person needs more information or has not given you any signs that they really can focus on your ask, then the seesaw goes down. If you are really stuck and it could go either way, here is one of my favorite questions to ask; I call it my "inclination test:"

> *Laura, when and if you were ready to* [fill this in: *invest with us, make a transformational gift, join our team, have the discussion with your mother-in-law about drawing up a will, ask your teenager to get a job, or explore alternative care with your doctor*] *what would that look like?*

I love this question because it resolves the inclination question along with so much more. The first part is using the person's name or title. When anyone hears their name they wake up, and now it is time to move quickly to get to the transformational question. The second part is *when and if.* That expression lets the person know that you are interested in their timing. If they respond, "I have no idea, I haven't given it any thought" the person needs more education; so you go back and provide more information. If the person says, "Gee, I always thought I would do *x*," then you know the person is ready because they have been giving this much thought.

The third part is your *ask without sounding like an ask.* In the preceding example—"when and if you were ready to invest with us"—in essence you made the ask: Invest with us. Now all you have to do is fill in the level of the investment and you have your ask. The fourth part, "What would that look like?" gets the person to visualize. The very words "look like" give the person the opportunity to visually imagine what that investment would look like.

The fifth part of this formula is assets. If your ask is for money, you should have some idea that the person can give you money. Again, as stated in item 5 regarding the reasons people do not like to ask, if you think the person can support you but you don't know the exact amount, take the first ask opportunity and say "I have no idea if you can do this" and then state the specific amount. If the person has previously shared with you that they have invested *x* amount with another company or person, then you should be pretty certain that they can make the same level or larger with you.

8. YOU HAVE NEVER GIVEN THE SIZE AMOUNT YOU NEED TO ASK. There was a time when we used a very old fundraising rule: You could not ask for an amount if you had not already given that exact amount. For example, if you were asking for $100,000, then you yourself needed to have given $100,000. While this was an admirable rule, it quickly faded because many volunteers in leadership positions could not make the size gift or investment

that the organization needed. So here is the way I resolve this issue. Anyone can ask for an amount that is much larger than what they could do *if* they ask the right way. The word to use is *stretch*, and this is how it is used:

> *Bill, I've made a stretch investment with the company, and I hope you will join me with an investment of x.*

> *Casey, I've made a stretch gift to this organization that I love, and I hope you will join me with a gift of x.*

Even if the person asks you the exact amount that you gave or invested, you can look them in the eye and be perfectly honest. Your amount was a stretch for you. By that I mean that you gave or invested with an amount that was larger than you originally thought possible. It tells them and shows them your commitment to the ask.

9. THE PERSON YOU WANT TO ASK GETS ASKED ALL THE TIME. We call this "tripping over the big fish." Every town, every region, every state, every nation has them—the known philanthropists and investors that people line up to approach. Remember when people discovered that Bill and Melinda Gates and Warren Buffet had money to give and invest? Practically every nonprofit requested a grant, and every company wanted to align with them. Next came the big start-ups in Silicon Valley who found themselves being showered with requests to be honored at a gala or given an award. Now, it's any successful entrepreneur. But let's say you want to approach one of these high-profile people because they may be a good fit for your ask. I believe honesty wins the day. I would be right up front and say:

> *Ms. Wonderful, we know you get many, many requests, but we truly believe we have an opportunity that is perfectly aligned with your key interests. We do not take lightly that we may be a long shot to get your attention and consideration but we promise it will be well worth your time. Would you be willing to meet with us for 15 minutes?*

THE ASK—it's two sentences and a question.

10. THE PRESUMPTION THAT THE PERSON YOU ARE ASKING DOES NOT HAVE THAT KIND OF MONEY. Presumptions can kill us! Before we even pick up the telephone or send an e-mail or text, we are off to the races in our minds that the person we want to ask doesn't really have that kind of money so why bother. This is what I call the *presumptive projection*. It happens most frequently in two situations: (1) we want to ask the people we are close to but protect them from being asked if we sense they may not have the assets and, (2) we make a quick judgment about the person's ability to give money without having a conversation.

For the people who are close, we project that it is not good to ask them for money now. Perhaps their children are in expensive private schools, someone lost their job, their father needs to be placed in a nursing home, a child needs to go to boarding school, or they have been rejected for additional health insurance. Or we may read that a person we want to engage and ask just got a divorce, their company has laid off 100 employees, or he or she has invested heavily elsewhere.

When you find yourself in this situation, very honestly ask yourself this question: "Are the facts deterring you, or are you projecting that if *you* were in these situations you would not want to give or invest?" The projection comes and starts with *you*. You instantly put yourself in their shoes; in essence you become them and then you make decisions for them with that person having never been asked!

Again it is *how you ask* with all the sensitivity in the world that makes this all possible. My suggestion, and it has worked for me, is to say:

> *Leslie, I cannot imagine what you are going through right now; your strength is beyond comprehensible. I've been working on/involved with a few projects that, even though the time might not be ideal, I think you would really want to be involved with at some level. If this is not a good time, please let me know; otherwise may I have the opportunity to share this with you?*

11. THE SURPRISE RESPONSE THAT WILL CATCH YOU OFF GUARD. Will you be caught off guard when you ask? Of course you will, time

and time again. That is part of the asking learning process. The more responses you hear, the better your asks become. In Chapter 4, we will go into great depth about how you can prepare for all the responses you may hear and how to respond. As a teaser, here is a story about one of my craziest responses and how I addressed it.

I was in charge of a very large capital campaign. When the time was right, we had a meeting with a trustee whom everyone loved and admired. He had been a trustee for over a decade. When we asked for a $2 million gift to help kick off the success of the campaign, an amount that matched exactly what he wanted to fund for the campaign, he put his hands behind his head, slid down the seat, and said, "What makes you think I have that kind of money?" I was blown away. What do you say to that? We all knew each other so well. The person who did the ask with me was someone our trustee knew, liked, and trusted. What one could have said was, "Well, we've researched you over these years and we know you have the assets," but that is *not* what you want to say. Instead, I said, "We have no idea if you can do this size investment, but you know *you* are the one everyone looks up to and admires to make this campaign a success." He left abruptly, and we thought this $2 million gift opportunity would never happen. Three days later he called me and said, "I'm in."

The moral of the story is to make your ask *regardless* of the response you think you will hear. Every response is a moment to perfect your ask.

12. KNOWING THE EXACT WORDS YOU SHOULD USE WHEN MAKING AN ASK. I have to admit I struggled with this many times. You meet people you want to ask, and in your head you keep hearing "But I know they want to hear certain words" and you can't find them so you don't ask. Well, I'm here to tell you there are no magic words, but there are words you can use that will mirror their tempo and sensibility and will resonate with the person you're asking. In Chapter 5 I will synthesize this for you. It is all about active listening and selecting words you are comfortable with using and that you feel will resonate with the person you wish to ask.

13. THE POSSIBILITY THAT THE PERSON WILL GIVE YOU IN TIME WHAT YOU WANT WITHOUT ASKING FOR IT. I call this *the ask without the ask*. Then I tell everyone that the ask without the ask will result in no money or tremendous disappointment that you did not get what you wanted. This happens in three situations: (1) you feel so close to the person that you believe they will naturally know what you want and do it; (2) you overthink every angle of the ask and so much time goes by that it will miraculously come up at some point in your conversation; and (3) you have engaged and cultivated the person so much that your actions are your way of asking. Avoid all three of these mindsets and activities at all costs.

You do more harm than good when you assume, procrastinate, or overextend yourself in activities without speaking about your ask. You send mixed messages when you do these things and they totally confuse the person. I was with an attorney who was doing very well at his firm but, naturally, wanted more clients. So during a reception I asked him how things were going. He said really well; he had just booked a country club for the day, invited all his present clients, and "they never put their hand in their wallet" the entire time. I said that's terrific and then asked him if he had the chance to chat with them one on one to ask them to send him some people who may need his services. He looked at me quite surprised and said, "I didn't need to. They got the message." Months later I spoke with him and asked him how many new clients he had gotten from that event? I think you know the ending of this story without me telling you: none. So I coached him to remember one unique thing about each person or something they said and then call them and say,

> *Thanks so much for your valuable time at the club. I recalled that you* (something unique about them/something they said) *mentioned your daughter was visiting college campuses—my niece is doing the same thing. Can we get together and compare notes? I'd love another perspective on this important decision.*

Then at the meeting, once the attorney had established a stronger rapport with each prospective client, I told him to share a *short* story about the work he does and then ask for the business.

Don't leave the ask to chance or think time or actions will fill in for your ask.

14. YOU ASKED THIS PERSON BEFORE. IT DID NOT GO WELL, BUT YOU HAVE A NEW PROJECT THAT IS PERFECT FOR THEM. What I like about this situation is the determination. Imagine that you asked someone for something and it did not go well, but you want to go back with another idea. Bravo! Here is an example of taking on this kind of risk but getting great results. A Broadway producer was in my class, and when it came time for the role playing with an ask he needed to do, I said OK, cue up the class. He said that he had asked a wealthy businesswoman who loved theater and that she had invested in two previous plays and both times the plays had a short run and closed. Her investments never yielded a return. He was working on a new play and he was most certain that the theme of the play would resonate with her core principles that she shared with him many times.

I must say he did an amazing role-play ask. He first told her she had every right to be disappointed in the past plays and he was very grateful to have her precious time. Next he outlined in one sentence the theme of the play and with tremendous enthusiasm stated that it matched her most important values and beliefs. Last and for the grand finale, he asked her for a $20 million investment and said that he wanted her as his key partner.

You now see how two sentences and a question can even be applied when you have the urge to win someone over; explain the past, state that it is a perfect match because you listened carefully to the person's values, and then make the bold ask. So what did our lady investor say? She said she would give him $10 million to start and that he better not blow this one. When and if she was convinced the play would do well, she might give more.

If you truly feel that you have a wonderful opportunity for someone but they either have turned you down before or were unsatisfied with previous results from prior asks, do make the ask. My caveat is to be on your guard not to overexplain the past or exaggerate the new offer.

15. THE PERSON YOU WANT TO ASK IS A MUCH BETTER ASKER THAN YOU.
I was consulting with a very well-known nonprofit, and one of our
prospects was a very well-known hedge-fund owner and philanthropist. He had never made a gift to this organization, but we
have heard from several reliable sources that he loved our mission.
I wanted the president or a trustee of the organization to make the
call and see our hedge-fund prospect, but they wanted someone on
the staff to see him first and determine whether he was really
interested. If he was interested, they would follow up. From the
start I did not think this was the best approach, because I believe
that in this instance and someone of this stature, you may only get
one chance to see. Be that as it may, it was my job to prepare a staff
member to get the appointment with him. She was terrified. He
had a reputation of being very unpredictable in meetings and worst
yet, he was a superior asker. You don't get to be in his shoes
without asking and winning at the game.

We worked on what the staff person would say if she had a 15-
minute meeting, a 20-minute meeting, or a 30-minute meeting. I
felt like I was back at the attorney general's office practicing my
oral argument at the Court of Appeals for the Third Circuit. You
stand in front of a podium with three lights on it—green, amber,
and red. The moment the red light comes on you are dismissed,
and any word you utter will not be considered part of your
argument. What terrified my staff person the most was that our
hedge-fund man would know she was there to eventually get
money from him. She also worried that he would press her into a
corner and demand she make the ask. So we practiced that many
times over.

She did get the meeting and it did last 15 minutes. There was
no small talk at all. He told her to get right to it, so she made the
ask and she did it well. He turned her down immediately, and
barely made eye contact with her as he was focused on some
documents on his desk. He said he had people who could do the
same thing we were asking for at a 10th of the price. She countered
that he had the first shot, and since he was turning it down, this
project was so important to the organization that we would turn to
other supporters. Well that got him. He demanded to know the
names, and she refused for confidentiality purposes. She closed

with saying he and his company would have been perfect for this gift, and if he changed his mind to let her know within the week. I was so proud of her, and she felt like, well, $15 million bucks, our ask price. Later, we were fortunate enough to meet a person who loved the project and agreed to fund the costs. We heard that our hedge-fund man was furious. I have to admit we were silently happy when we heard that news.

Even if you know or have heard that the person you want to ask is a better asker, ask anyway. You will always walk away with more self-esteem because you did it, and I guarantee it will be quite the learning experience.

So there you have it, 15 reasons why people do not ask but now *you* know how to overcome each one if and when they should arise. You have nothing to lose and everything to gain. Don't let one of these reasons stand in the way of your happiness and your success.

PART

II

How Should You Ask?

How to Be an Exceptional Asker

'M OFTEN ASKED, WHAT DOES IT TAKE TO be a really good asker? I thought about this and said, "Well, why would anyone want to be good when they can be exceptional?" I often say to clients, "Sure I can get you to 'great' but wouldn't you want to get to 'exceptional?'" So I put together those characteristics, those qualities I have observed over the years that I believe make someone an exceptional asker. Now I want you to be that exceptional asker, and I can get you there. You could have the time to be a good or great asker, but why not put in a little extra time to be that exceptional asker? Here are the characteristics I aspire to and practice in preparation for each ask.

THE 10 ESSENTIAL CHARACTERISTICS OF AN EXCEPTIONAL ASKER

Before I share the techniques to use when you make your asks, it is important that you know the characteristics that epitomize the exceptional asker. These are qualities that I believe everyone should strive for, adopt, and exercise whenever you make your ask. So here we go. Askers need to:

- Believe 100 percent in their ask.
- Speak with both passion and compassion.
- Listen to each and every word.
- Prepare for how the person will react to the ask.
- Take the time to do the ask in person.
- Treat each ask as a special moment in time.

- Be mindful of body language, dress, and tone of voice.
- Follow up with each ask until there is an answer.
- Thank the person regardless of the response.
- Embrace that the win is that you made the ask, not the result.

Throughout this book you have read that if you do not believe 100 percent in your ask, why should anyone else? I have observed many asks that fizzled out because the person's tone of voice was weak, their body language reflected their lack of confidence, they never looked the person in the eye at the moment of the ask, they became distracted with objects around the room, and in short they just were not *present* during the ask. Because you may have only one opportunity to ask any one person, you should repeat over and over to yourself that you deserve it, it will go well, and that you just cannot wait to make someone's day. Positive energy will draw the person to you, and you are halfway to getting what you want.

Speaking with passion and compassion is always an attractive and alluring characteristic. Think of all the great speeches, inspirational moments, and life lessons that you have heard and admire. What comes to mind for me are the words and the charismatic energy of Martin Luther King, Jr.; John F. Kennedy; Maya Angelou; Oprah Winfrey; and Tony Robbins. What comes to mind for you? When you speak from the heart, you let the person know that you are genuine, you care about them, and that you selected them to be a part of your next chapter in life. That for sure will draw them closer to you, and they will carefully listen to every word of your ask. Note that I used the terms "passion" and "compassion," leading with "passion." Be careful not to be overly dramatic when speaking and sharing your compassion about others or important causes.

Let me expand upon this through an illustration. I was working with an animal-rights group with dedicated and amazing volunteers. When it came time to explain the work they do with potential supporters, they were very heavy-handed on the compassion side, almost to the point that it made the person listening feel guilty. See if you can detect the difference between these two asks:

1. *I love animals, all animals, and yet horrible people do horrible things to helpless animals. I want to shower them with the love and attention that they never received and tell everyone I meet that they should adopt one of these precious creatures. Have you or someone you know adopted a rescued animal?*

2. *My passion to rescue abused animals has led me to work for this important group. I am so lucky to work with volunteers every day who are dedicated to the compassionate work it takes to rescue abused animals and bring them into safe and loving families. Have you or someone you know adopted a rescued animal?*

I think you see how being overly compassionate can really turn off some people and deflect them from your ask. This is why it is very important that you find a balance between passion and compassion.

The art of listening can sometimes seem to be a dying art. How many conversations have you been in when you wondered to yourself, "Did they hear anything I had to say?" Well unfortunately, when you make an ask, it can have the same result. A good rule for you to follow is: *There is more power in listening than in talking.* When you ask for anything, you have to keep it tight and simple. I have been with co-askers who felt it was necessary to give the person every excruciating detail, beginning with when they developed the idea and proceeding to the challenges and disasters and the comments from other people on the product—and we haven't even gotten to the ask. Of course, it is important for the person to know about the details of your ask. However, you do not have to front-load the conversation so that the only person speaking is you. This is why my formula for the ask consists of two sentences and a question. I end the ask with a question so that the next person to speak is the person you asked. That invites a dialogue, an even exchange of conversation. When the person is engaged, you have their buy-in, and now they are part of your process, not just a spectator listening to you.

I will share with you that listening was very hard for me at first. My runaway enthusiasm unfortunately gave little room for the other person to speak or contribute. So here are three techniques that I use to keep myself a better listener:

1. I put my hands down, close to my chair. When I speak I know I use my hands a lot, and if I slow down my hands it signals me to listen.

2. In every two sentences I ask a question; that clears the path for the person to speak.

3. The more I speak, the less I will get. That one is a real motivator for me. I say in my classes, "Once you have asked, if you continue speaking you will not get what you want." That's motivation enough to stay silent.

I think if you did a word search throughout this book you would find the word "prepare" or "preparation" as one of the most used words. Why? Because preparation wins the day! There is no shortcut to the preparation you will need to do for any ask. We will go into great detail on this topic further along in this chapter, but for now, know that an exceptional asker is one who always prepares.

The next characteristic of an exceptional asker is one of my favorites. Take the time to do your asks *in person*. Yes, it is far easier to send a text, e-mail, or written proposal or to make a telephone call. But here is my rule, and I hope this catches your attention and that you follow it. *You have a 75 percent greater chance of getting what you want if you ask in person.* How did I come up with that statistic? It is based purely on my experiences. Put yourself in the shoes of the person you want to ask. If you were asked via e-mail (or worse, a group e-mail), a text, or a voice mail, how special would you feel? Not very special, I imagine, because asking in those ways sends the signal that you are not special, it does not matter whether you agree or not, and there will be others to ask.

Now let's reverse the scenario. If someone sends an e-mail or text or makes a call to set up a time to meet with you in person at your convenience to discuss an opportunity that may be of great interest to you, how would you feel? I imagine that now you sense the person took the time to contact you and to meet with you, so it must be important. You probably have a greater tendency to meet with them. This is why your goal is to do as many asks as you can in person. Asking in person tells the person you want to ask "You are special," and "I gave this a lot of thought and selected you as someone who may want to be involved."

The one caveat I have to this rule is that the age of the person you want to ask may steer you in the direction to text your ask, not make your ask in person. Many people have shared with me that people who are in their 20s or 30s only liked to be asked via a text message. While this may be true, I would explore first the possibility if you can meet with a person in this age group to make your ask and if this young person only wants to hear about it via a text, then do it. I would still try to meet and do it in person but if that is not what the person wants, then ask away in your text message.

Asking in person sets up the next important characteristic—treating the ask as a special moment in time. This is your one chance to get exactly what you want, so why would you blow it? If you do not treat it as something special, a great opportunity, or a new chapter in your life, why should anyone listen? This characteristic is also directly tied with the first one—believing 100 percent in your ask. If you do, then you will naturally want to single this out as a special moment and not nonchalantly go through the motions during your ask. I will illustrate how important this is in Chapter 5, when we discuss The Five-Step Foolproof Method for Any Ask.

You can prepare and trim your ask down to two sentences and a question and then sabotage your ask by wearing inappropriate clothes, slouching in your seat, or speaking in a low or annoying tone of voice. Let's break these things down one by one so I can show you how important each one is to your ask presentation. There is no one way to dress when you make your ask, but I like to look professional regardless of the person I am asking. I'm not saying you have to wear a dress or a full suit and tie every time you ask, but if you are asking someone in business, I would certainly look as professional as possible. If you are asking a friend, relative, or colleague, I would always try to look as neat as I can in casual clothes. No wrinkles, tight clothes, worn shoes, or anything that would send the signal that you didn't think enough of this special moment to look your best, even in casual clothing. A word of caution about your dress is necessary here. Pay particular attention to ensure that your hair is styled nicely, you don't go overboard with jewelry, and that your makeup is not over the top. I know this may seem beyond obvious, but even people you know size you up in seconds and their judgment about you is based largely on what they see.

Pay particular attention to your body language during your ask. Do stand straight with your shoulders back and your head and eyes fixed squarely on the person you want to ask. That sends the signal that you are confident and convinced that your ask is worthy of their attention. Is your head tilting too much? Are you looking down or away, or are you fixated on your written materials? When you sit down, are you slouched back in the seat, or are you leaning too far forward or back? All these are visually distracting behaviors that will steal attention from the person listening to you.

Just as your body language can send either a great or a distracting message, your tone of voice can do the same. For instance, if the asker is nervous, she may tend to lower her voice, to cough in between sentences, or to get dry mouth and be desperate for a glass of water. Voice and body language go hand in hand. When someone lowers his voice, he also generally lowers his head. Now will it not only be difficult to hear what he is saying, but all eye contact will be lost as well. When you ask, your voice should be clear and convincing, neither forceful and overbearing nor so low and shaky that the person begins feeling sorry for you.

The tip I have for you is to record your ask on your smart phone several times and play it back. Do you like it? I do this periodically, and I'm amazed at what I catch. At one point, I was using the word "absolutely" way too many times. The other tip I have for you is to practice your ask in front of a mirror. What do you see? I saw that I had a wicked head tilt to the right that I would never have known had I not practiced in front of a mirror.

Have you ever heard the saying "The fortune is in the follow-up?" The meaning of this expression is that if you don't follow up, you most likely will not get the fortune you seek. My saying (and I know you are so surprised I have one) is "More money is left on the table because you did not follow up and receive an answer." The most common response to an ask is "I have to think about it." When you hear that response, you are almost to a yes. So many people interpret that this is a no and believe the person is putting you off until another time when they will actually say no. Treat this response as a yes, and do the follow-up steps until you have an answer. All too often we leave the ask meeting without having a definitive plan to follow up. So time goes by. A lot of time goes by, and before you know it the person you asked must be asked again because they forgot crucial elements in your ask.

Here are my tips for you to follow up:

- At the ask meeting, set up a time and date when you will speak again.
- Call the person the next day and thank them for their time.
- Send a handwritten thank you note that will reach them two days later.
- Offer to send more information or to have another investor or donor contact them so they can share their reasons for making the investment with you or making a gift to your organization.
- Mix up the communication and the communicator; vary who contacts the person and what to say.

Timing is everything when you follow up. Out of sight is out of mind. If you let too much time pass between your ask and your follow-up, you might as well begin all over again because the person has probably forgotten most of what you said. This is why I suggest you call them the next day and, if appropriate, send a handwritten note. Always offer to send more information and tailor it to meet the needs requested. You do not have to send everything, just the relevant pieces. If you have people you know, like, and trust who have invested with you or supported your organization and are willing to give a small testimony, then by all means offer to have them contact your prospect so they can share their experiences. The last tip—mix up the communication and mix up the communicator—is extremely important. It is very boring if Laura picks up the telephone and leaves messages every day or every other day saying "Hi, it's Laura. Is there anything we can do to help you reach a decision?" over and over again. So mix it up. Leave voice mail, send a text or e-mail where appropriate, or have someone else make the call.

It can be very difficult and very painful when you receive a no response to your ask, but here is where the exceptional asker shines. Regardless of what you hear after your ask, always, always say thank you. After all, the person did make time for you and deserves to hear a thank you. A "thank you" says that you are a class act, that there are no hard feelings, and that while it did not go in your favor, you still give thanks. You will see the value of this thank you in Chapter 6 when we discuss "Asking U-Turns." My rule here is "A no now does not mean a no later." The person did not say "No, never, there is no way on this earth I will ever do what you asked," but unfortunately that is what we hear when we get a no. So for now, just remember to always say thank you when the person answers your ask.

Last, but certainly not least, is the final characteristic of an exceptional asker—embracing that the *win* is that you made the ask, not the result. I know many of you right now are saying, "She's crazy—all this work to make the ask, and now we shouldn't care if we get a yes?" But that is not what I am saying. By focusing on the ask and not the result, you remove your anxiety about getting a yes. Remember in Chapter 3, "Why People Do Not Ask," one of the most frequent reasons why people do not ask is that they do not want to hear no or interpret the no as rejection. When you focus on making your exceptional ask, you won the minute you made it. This serves many purposes.

First, you will be concentrating very carefully on all the elements listed previously, such as believing 100 percent in your ask, speaking with passion and compassion, listening carefully, preparing the conversation, making sure you do your ask in person, and dressing appropriately while using convincing body language and tone of voice. Second, you spend the time you need to stay present during your ask and avoid the urge to get it over quickly so you get your response. Third, you will appear and sound more confident if you focus on the ask, knowing you may receive a yes, a maybe, or a no. Trust me; when you place your energy on the ask and not on the result, more positive results will come your way.

ACTIONS TO TAKE BEFORE YOU ASK

Now that we know the qualities that make a person an exceptional asker, let me share with you the actions to take before any ask. Your mental preparation before you make your ask will set up your success strategy. Think of the actions in the check list that follows. Make sure you check off each one before you make your ask. This will add laser focus to your ask and place you in the absolute best mental frame of mind when you ask.

- Be personal and sincere and use your own voice.
- Treat every ask separately and distinctly.
- Invest in your project or organization *before* you ask others to invest or give.
- Add relatives, friends, and colleagues to your list of potential investors and supporters.
- Determine the exact amount you want as well as the date when you want a decision.

In "10 Essential Characteristics of an Exceptional Asker," we detailed the importance of speaking with both passion and compassion and paying attention to body language, tone of voice, and attire. The first action step drills down a bit deeper. Sometimes we have a tendency to be so focused on how we look and what right words to use are that we may ignore feeling natural and relaxed. I do hope you do the exercises of recording your voice and practicing in front of the mirror; now add this further checkpoint. Make sure you feel good about how you look and sound. If there are particular words that resonate with you, use them. Whenever someone needs a few months or even a year to consider my ask, I like to say:

Thank you for considering this and letting me know the time frame that works for you. I will stay in good communication with you and then circle back so that we can keep this opportunity in the forefront of your consideration. Does that work for you?

I like to use *circle back* because that gives me the confidence and satisfaction that my ask is still alive, and now we are both on the same page as to when the person can take action on my ask. Select the words or phrases that work for you, and let your personality shine through. People are attracted to sincerity, and you will be in a much better position for people to consider your ask if you are sincere.

Diane was a young woman in my sales training session. She had her list of 1,000 clients—some good customers and some potential clients. I asked her to share with me how she stays in touch with her current clients. She said that she groups them in lists based on how much they have purchased. The highest-paying clients get more attention from her, more invitations, more webinars, and more e-newsletters. The clients with less business receive less attention. As a whole, this is not bad strategy because we should be paying attention to those clients who do more business with us. I asked Diane how she knew that her highest-paying clients *want* or *need* this level of attention. She didn't know—it was just her practice.

This gets to the heart of the second action step: Before the ask, treat your clients, customers, potential friends, relatives, or college supporters *separately* and *distinctly.* Your supporters and investors know whether they are getting something that is uniquely tailored for them or whether they are being lumped into a group that is receiving the same attention. Now with 1,000 clients and potential clients, this may seem like a ridiculous and impossible step to take. There simply may not be enough time in the world for you to do this with each client. However, I know how you can accomplish this very important step. From the outset, *before* you ask for the business, for the charitable gift, or for a neighbor to watch your house while you are on vacation, make a mental note and ask:

What is the best way we can show the value of your investment with us?

How can we fulfill your expectations when you make this meaningful and transformational gift?

How do we stay in good communication with each other, and how often would you like me to be in touch with you?

I learned to use this technique just a few years ago, and I absolutely love it, because it works. The person or company will let you know how *they* want to stay connected to you, and now you know the level of attention you need to give them. I have had some extremely wealthy donors tell me, "Just a call now and then is fine," when I might have reached out to them on a monthly basis because they were among my top donors. This is how you avoid the trap of lumping people and companies together solely by their level of investment or gifts. The same applies with friends, relatives, and colleagues. If you have asked them to help you out, ask them how you can stay in contact with them or how you can keep them informed as to how their act of kindness helped you. Avoid the temptation to *assume* people and companies need *x* attention. It is so much easier once you hear from them what they want and then give them the attention they request. That's how you treat everyone you ask separately and distinctly.

I was training a mid-sized nonprofit board and emphasizing how important it was that every board member needed to make a monetary gift before asking for money. One board member raised his hand and said that he had been on the board for nine years and had served on several committees and that was his "gift." I have heard this more times than I care to count. While I applaud and respect the volunteer hours that board members devote to deserving causes around the world, every board member needs to make a monetary gift to that nonprofit before he can ask for money.

I do not hold back on this advice. It is a horrible situation when a board member or anyone who needs to raise money asks for it and the person turns and says, "What did you give?" "How much did you invest?" You will receive zero from your that person if this question is raised and the asker has not given a monetary amount. Why should anyone give you money or support your cause if you, the asker, have not done so as well? You send the signal that it's OK for them to give, but you don't have to. That also diminishes all the principles that make up an exceptional asker.

The easiest way to address this (and the one that has worked for me) is to ask each board member to make a yearly stretch gift. I mentioned this stretch concept in Chapter 3. For some it may be $250; for others, $2,500; while for still others it may be $250,000 or more. Of course, these board asks should be done in person by the board chair and CEO or by the CEO and top development officers.

This action step of making an initial investment also applies to startup opportunities, sales asks, and everyday situations. If you are starting a new business, you naturally have startup costs, but in addition you should make an investment in your own company. When you ask for outside investors you can say:

In addition to the startup costs of x, I also put in x amount of my personal money. Your investment will join mine, and that will attract other investors. How do you feel about this solid investment plan?

If you are in sales, you can say:

I personally purchased the product (or additions to the product) and have used it for over a year. It has streamlined my business and eliminated the need for me to use three other applications. I'd be more than happy to share with you how this grew my business; can I show you now?

If you wanted another couple to join you for a vacation you could say:

We found a great beachfront condo with two bedrooms for the first week in August, as we discussed, and it's in our price range. I'm willing to put down the deposit now and we can split the expenses, including the deposit, when we get the bill. How does all that sound to you?

Make your initial investment first before you ask. It gives you the added confident advantage because you took the first investment step. Nothing can stop you because now this is not just an idea or a wish; your ask has *you* as the initial backer.

There is always a moment in my sessions when a person lets me know that they simply cannot ask their friends, relatives, colleagues, or business partners for money, to volunteer, or to attend an event. When I ask why, the response is usually "it will feel awkward" or "it will jeopardize the relationship." I understand completely; I truly do. No one wants to put a person who is close to them on the spot or anticipate that the ask will change the dynamic of their strong personal connection.

As we saw in Chapter 2, asking mantra number two, "When you ask for money you are not taking something away, you are giving an opportunity." Asking the people closest to you will never alienate them if you ask in the right way. Quite the opposite will happen. If you *don't* ask them, then they will feel alienated because they know you are asking other people. They sense that there is a circle of people better, richer, smarter, and more important to you and they are not in it. Many people do not believe me when I say this, but I have queried many people who were not asked, and they respond that the person who asked them knows "better" people. Think about this: The people closest to you know what boards you are on; they know where you volunteer and whether you have to raise money and that part of your role is to attend events and bring guests. When you don't ask them, they think that they are not needed and that you have this circle of wealthy folks whom you tap when you need help. So the action step before you ask is to make sure that people who are closest to you are on your list to be asked.

When you are ready to ask them, here is how you can do it without putting anyone on the spot and without changing the relationship:

*Jim, as you know, I have been on this community board for a few years, and we have our signature fundraising event next fall. **I have no idea** whether you are interested in learning more and possibly attending. Are you interested; if so I can share some details with you?*

*Emma, as of September 20, I'm in charge of staffing the registration booth for our walk against cancer. **I have no idea** whether this interests you, but I wanted to extend the invitation for you to help out as a volunteer. If you are interested would you want me to share the information with you now?*

*Liam, I believe you know that I started my boutique personal training business just a few months ago. **I have no idea** whether you may know* *some people who may want to come out for a free session and learn more about my business model. Is this something we can talk about now?*

The key is to say *"I have no idea"* which sets the ask up to be a light invitation to talk about your opportunity. It is their chance to say yes or no. This is a very gentle yet inclusive way to involve the people who are closest to you with what you need. Best of all, it works. I've seen this go very smoothly, and I'm most certain it will work for you. Just remember the *last* thing you want to do is alienate someone you like or love because you didn't include them on the list to be asked and then you didn't ask them.

The last action step is the one that many people find the hardest. They prepare for the ask but they do not have a definitive ask amount. The ask comes out sounding like this:

Mason, thanks so much for your time. We talked about your company buying five more pallets of sheet rock. Did you decide what you want to do?

What is glaringly missing here? Both the price and the date when you want Mason to make a decision. Here are other examples where the amount and dates are absent:

Christine, we have spoken previously about you joining our committee. We think you would be a fantastic addition. What do you think?

Charles, we talked last week about your availability to cover our soccer practice next month when I'm away for business. The team will be happy to know we don't have to cancel it if you say yes. So can you?

Madeline, you and your family have been so generous to our organization and we thank you. We have been discussing your increased end-of-year gift. Have you been able to discuss it with your family and reach a decision?

All these examples may sound like great asks, but they are missing the key ingredients of a specific amount and a specific date. When you are planning your asks and practicing, I hope you make sure you include both. Here is how your asks should go:

Mason, thanks so much for your time. We talked about your company buying five more pallets of sheet rock that would cost $1,500. Can you *let us know by May 1 so we can guarantee shipment on time, which we know is important to your company?*

Christine, we have spoken previously about you joining our committee. We think you would be a fantastic addition. Can you let us know by next Friday because that's when we will be putting together our meeting notice, and we want to include you on our letterhead?

Charles, we talked last week about your availability to cover our soccer practice next month when I'm away for business. The team will be happy to know we don't have to cancel it if you say yes. Can you let me know by next Monday?

Madeline, you and your family have been so generous to our organization, and we thank you. We have been discussing your consideration of an increased end-of-year $5,000 gift by December 15 of this year, which would allow us to continue our good work. Have you been able to discuss it with your family and reach a decision?

I think you can see how crystal clear these asks are and also how helpful this information can be to the person you want to ask. Everyone will be on the same page as to the amount you want and when you want a decision. You will see how important this action step is in the Chapter 5, "The Five-Step Foolproof Method for Any Ask."

While taking these action steps before an ask may seem obvious, and you may be saying to yourself, "Of course I would do these things," in reality many people do not take the time to prepare for them *before* they ask. Be that exceptional asker; take these steps before asking. Watch your success rate skyrocket!

THREE QUESTIONS THAT COME BEFORE ANY ASK

If I had an hour minutes to solve a problem and my life depended on it, I'd spend the first 55 minutes determining the proper question to ask, for once I know the proper question, I could solve the problem in less than five minutes.

Albert Einstein[1]

---

[1] Quoted in David Sturt and Todd Nordstrom, "Are You Asking The Right Question?", *Forbes*, Oct 18, 2013. Available at https://www.forbes.com/sites/davidsturt/2013/10/18/are-you-asking-the-right-question/#19d361db76c5.

Einstein knew the importance of questions. Questions are powerful, and if you use them as preparation for your ask they become a game changer. You can use my three questions that come before any ask when you don't have too much time to prepare. Of course you know that I want you to prepare as much as you can before you ask. However, sometimes you find yourself on the spot, or someone calls you and wants to meet that day and it is your golden opportunity to make your ask. When that happens, use these three questions to prepare your ask. In Chapter 5 I will give you my "Five-Step Foolproof Method for Any Ask" that you can use when you have more time.

Here are the three questions that you should anticipate a person will ask you whenever you ask:

1. Why me?
2. Why now?
3. What will it do?

If you can, put yourself in the shoes of the person you want to ask, ask and answer these questions out loud. Then you are perfectly prepared even when you do not have a lot of time to prepare. Let me show you how this works. Let's say you meet a friend for lunch and she asks you, "How is your new business going?" You start to share with her that you have been calling potential investors to meet with them and that things are looking really good. She turns to you and says, "How much are you looking for? I may be interested." I have to take a minute here and show you that when you hear that question or any variation of it, that is your *invitation to ask*.

People leave clues, and we miss every one of them.

When someone says, "What can I do?" or "What do you need?" or "I may be interested; how much is it?" that is your signal to jump right in and ask. What happens more often is that you skip over this clue and start to explain more about the project, more about what you need—more details, but you never ask. As I said earlier in this chapter, when you are the exceptional asker you are the superior listener. Listen for these clues, and do not be afraid to ask when you hear them.

So when your friend says, "How much are you looking for?" think for a few seconds about the three questions: Why her? Why now? What will it do? That will frame your response to her question, and it will frame your ask. You can say,

> *I would love to have you as an early investor, and your timing could not be more perfect. If I can raise the initial $300,000 this month, not only will it cover the production costs, but it will also attract future investors. I've invested $100,000; would you consider investing $50,000 this month so that together we can reach $300,000?*

Look at how these two sentences and a question answered each of the three modeled questions.

- Why me? Having your friend as an early investor would be ideal.
- Why now? This emphasizes the importance of raising the money this month.
- What will it do? Reaching the goal of $300,000 would cover production costs and attract new investors.

Use these three questions if you are ever put on the spot and you need to ask. Remember to be that superior listener because you don't want to be the one who skips over the clues. If you do, your ask gets delayed, and as we all know, time is money!

While I am writing this book I am in development to create a new show that will either be on television or on an app. Yes, very exciting! One thing that we are looking into is having a brand sponsor. After all, creating, producing, and airing a show for any medium costs money. Before we approach any company to be our brand partner, I worked to answer these three questions, anticipating that our prospective brand partner would ask them.

First, why me, or in this instance, why this company? The answer to this first question is that we have carefully researched companies that support charities locally, nationally, and internationally because the show will feature nonprofits locally, nationally, and internationally. This would make the company a natural fit. The second question is always a hard one to answer, and it is the one that most people skip over. Why now? That question addresses timing. Why does it have to be done now? I like to answer this by stating my goal and working backwards. I ask myself, what won't happen if it does not get done now? In my example, we want to be the first one to have the show that can raise the awareness of the work of many charities, work through the issues that are preventing them from raising more money, give the viewers an opportunity to give while entertaining them along the way. You will see how you can use this technique more extensively in Chapter 5.

Additionally this second question—Why now?—can be addressed with the following advice. I highly recommend that when you ask, you should instill a sense of urgency. Notice I said *urgency*, not *emergency*. No one likes to be put on the spot and feel as though they have to bail you out immediately because you are in a tight situation. You can instill a sense of urgency by simply explaining why you feel the time is right for what you want to do. In my example, I would say: "The timing could not be more perfect, because right now the world is turning to nonprofits to make a bigger impact and address the unsolved needs of people and causes. Government funding anywhere is all but gone, but great corporate citizens like your company can have the ideal opportunity to be known as the charity crusader. This show would give tremendous exposure to a variety of audiences, and wouldn't you agree we need to do that now?" That is how you speak about and describe a sense of urgency. It is very powerful and very persuasive if you can position your ask as a call to action, and answering the question, "Why now?" will do that for you.

The last question, "What will it do?" is where you can talk about your vision—your motivation for your ask and how it will affect lives and bring about change. If you can quantify the impact, that would be fantastic. In my example I would say, "This show will skyrocket the awareness of great charities around the world and inspire viewers to support them. It will also do something no other show has done—reveal in dozens of ways how any charity can overcome any obstacle and emerge as the change agent locally, nationally, and internationally. Wouldn't you agree this is a first-of-its-kind show, one that can make a global impact?"

If I wanted to add some metrics to this example, I might say, "The first year of the show we will focus on seven very diverse charities that need to tackle an internal or external major problem in order to raise awareness and money. We anticipate that each charity's revenue will increase by at least 15 percent and that our viewers will even want to volunteer for some of these groups. Wouldn't you agree that increasing charitable revenue and volunteerism will have a global impact?"

Test it out. Try asking these three questions and answering them for any ask you need to make. If you need to ask a friend to recommend a medical specialist, you could say:

I know you have used many specialists and you seem so happy with each one. I need a good dermatologist right away to check out some things that have been troubling me. Can you recommend one so that I can stop worrying?

It's as simple as that. All three questions were answered.

Another example might be that if you want a promotion at work, you could say:

As my boss, you know that I have been the interim director for six months, fulfilling all the responsibilities of the director position that has been vacant. I would like you to consider giving me the title of director now, because it will demonstrate to our internal and external constituencies that everything is flowing smoothly and that our team is solid and productive. Will you consider giving me this title effective January 1?

These three questions also help you to focus your ask while not being tempted to describe and over-describe what you want to the point of distracting the person you are asking. Keep it simple, tight, and focused, and the person you are asking will most definitely appreciate it.

In the following chapter I will share with you my "Five-Step Foolproof Method for any Ask." You can use this when you have more time to prepare your ask. So now you have the three questions to ask when you have limited time to prepare. THE ASK—we've got you covered!

The 5-Step Foolproof Method for Any Ask

WE ARE AT THE HEART OF THIS BOOK IN this chapter. Read it, re-read it, take notes, or put tabs on the pages, because this chapter is the playbook to your asking success. As I stated in the preface, I have put *organization, structure, and focus* on the ask, and you will see in this chapter exactly what that means. If you follow the steps I lay out here and practice them with any ask you need to make, you will be abundantly amazed at what you can get. I must say this part of the book is a personal favorite of mine. If you remember anything in this book or need to highlight anything in this book, this is the place to do it. I created this process a few years ago, and I use it in all my asks. Throughout my years of listening and observing the way people have asked for such things as an upgrade to their travel arrangements, advice on financial retirement, more cooperation from their children, or a salary increase, I discovered that if they had only followed these five steps, they would have gotten exactly what they wanted.

These five steps do take more time and more preparation than the three questions that come before any ask that we saw in Chapter 4, but trust me; they are worth it. This is where my organization, structure, and focus model really comes into play. These five steps are very structured, and they should be followed in order—no skipping here! I like to say that each step is a box. Once you have done step 1, check it off, then move on to step 2. That's where the structure comes into focus. I find that people are willing to give this a try because there is structure to this process. So here are the five steps:

1. Know exactly what you want, with numbers and dates.
2. Prepare the conversation.

3. Deliver with confidence.

4. Clarify what you think you heard.

5. Plan your next move at the ask.

KNOW EXACTLY WHAT YOU WANT

Let's take these steps one by one. You first have to know exactly what you want, with numbers and dates. Most people know what they want, such as a better hotel room, more money for retirement, their children to clean their room, or a salary increase. That's a great start, but without numbers and dates, your ask is weak. You could get a better hotel room, but unless you state that you do not want to pay extra, you will get the room but at a cost you do not want. You could get more money for retirement, but it may be through financial vehicles that are too risky for you. You could get your children to clean their room, but that may be once a month when you want it every day. You could get a salary increase, but that may not be until next year. Now you see the importance of adding numbers and dates to your ask. Using these examples, this is how you check off step 1:

> *I want an upgrade to my hotel room reservation tonight at no additional cost to me.*
>
> *I want to have an additional $50,000 each year when I retire in three years and avoid high-risk planning vehicles.*
>
> *I want my children to clean their rooms every day by 6:00 PM.*
>
> *I want a $10,000 raise effective January 1.*

There is a real difference between knowing what you want and knowing what you want with numbers and dates.

Another factor in knowing exactly what you want is *why you want it*. Why is it important to you? We have all heard the expression "what's your why?" and this is where that expression has exponential meaning. When people cannot articulate their why, I ask them "What *won't* happen if you don't get what you want?" Once you start listing what won't happen, you can crystallize your why. For example, if you do not get the upgrade to your room, you may never go back to the hotel and also tell your friends not to go there. If you don't get an additional $50,000 in your retirement years, you may have to move and severely alter the lifestyle you currently enjoy. If your children do not clean their room by 6:00 PM each night, they do not get to play with their friends on Saturday. If you do not receive your $10,000 raise, you will start looking for a new job.

Now that you have what *won't* happen, I reverse those reasons and put them into a positive spin. It goes like this:

I selected your hotel because of the location and the design of the rooms. I have a heavy work load and many back-to-back business meetings. Could you check for me whether I could have an upgrade to a suite at no additional cost so that I can do some of my meetings in my room?

We thought carefully about this and we want to do everything now to ensure that we can maintain our lifestyle when we retire. With your help I'm sure we can figure out how we can save or earn an additional $50,000 a year. What have you done for your other clients who wanted the same as we do?

Listen kids, it's not your favorite thing to do but I need you to clean your room each day by 6:00 PM, and this is why. If your room is a mess, your life, family, friends, and everything about you is a mess, and I know that is not what you want. So what do you say, can you clean your room so that we can have more fun on the weekends?

Each of these examples explains the *why*—why you want what you ask. Add this to step 1 and it's bonus time!

Let me show you exactly how practical step 1 can be. I was speaking in Washington, D.C., and had a lot of work, as we all do, before and after this speaking engagement. I thought on the train ride in, if I had a spacious room I could feel more creative, not as though I were in a hermetically sealed hotel room. So I got to the hotel (a very upscale one, I might add), and they gave me my room. I have a routine about hotel rooms. When I arrive at the room, I keep my luggage on me and open the door and see whether I like it. Inevitably, despite my telling them at the front desk and having on my hotel record that I do not want to be by an elevator or an ice or vending machine, I get the room by the elevator or the vending or ice machine. I seem to have this happen to me a lot with hotel rooms. Well on this occasion, that did not happen, but I got a room where the desk was practically in the bathroom—no joke. It was literally in the hallway from the bedroom to the bathroom. With key in hand I returned to the front desk. You could see that my initial check-in person was worried, but another person asked me if they could help. I explained the layout of the room and how I really needed some space because I was there for three days and would be in the room a great deal of the time.

He looked at me and pulled out a piece of paper and two pens. He drew a tic-tac-toe diagram on the sheet of paper. He said to me, "Here's the deal. If you win the tic-tac-toe game, you get the room upgrade." Game on. I smiled, took the pen, and put a great big X in the center square. Now if you play or have ever played tic-tac-toe, you know that when you make this move, you win every time. My hotel check-in person played along until I won. Then he said, you won and gave me new keys to a new room. I thanked him and went to my new room. It was a palatial suite, three times the size of the room I had, with an office space, a divan, and a bathroom with a Jacuzzi. I was so excited I called him from the room phone to thank him. He answered and asked if I liked the room? I said, as Princess of Tic-Tac-Toe, yes! Step 1—it works; now get your hotel upgrade.

PREPARE THE CONVERSATION

We can check off box 1 happily, and we are ready to go to box 2—prepare the conversation. This is the step that most people skip, or if they do prepare, they do so in their heads. The first rule of this step is that you must *write down* at least 15 responses you think you will receive to your ask. That's right—at least 15 and in writing! It is really not that hard to do, so let me get you started with my list. You can then select the ones you think you will hear. The great thing about this list is that you can add to it when someone gives you a response you have never heard. Then that response goes on the list. This is an all-out effort to have you prepared and ready to respond when they answer your ask. Here are the most common responses I have received to my asks or have heard from others about responses to their asks:

- "I have to think about it."
- "That is a lot of money."
- "Why are you asking me?"
- "Can I do this at a later time?"
- "This is all I am authorized to give."
- "I need more information."
- "I have to speak to other people before I can make this decision."
- "Can I do this over time?"
- "Who else is supporting you?"
- "Why is this so important to you?"
- "What did you give?"
- "Does 100 percent of your board/staff give?"
- "I invested with you already; why do you need more?"
- "Your projections are way off. How did you come up with this valuation?"
- "What makes you think I have this kind of money?"
- "I already gave you a bonus last year. Why do you feel you need a raise?"
- "We don't make these kinds of exceptions for our guests."
- "Why do you need to spend more time with your family; what about us?"
- "Do you really think we need to invite x number of guests for this event?"
- "After you ask other people, then come to me."
- "That's as high as I can go."
- "I supported your event. Why do I need to make an additional gift?"
- "I can't help you, but you should speak to x about this."
- "What will happen if you don't get the money you need?"
- "I'm sorry, I just can't."

Now notice that none of these responses *appear* to be positive responses, yet many are. "I have to think about it" is a wonderful positive response, bringing you almost to a yes. "I have to speak with other people" is also almost to a yes because the person is giving your ask so much consideration that they want to get the opinion of other decision makers. So while you are listing the responses you think you will hear, be sure to list the ones that are a direct yes as well. In my experience, when people hear a yes to their ask, that is where the *real* surprise occurs. The first reaction (and the incorrect assumption I might add) is that if the person said yes right away, you did not ask for enough.

I shake my head when I hear this. Please erase this thinking. You thought long and hard about your ask, you prepared and delivered it perfectly, and you got what you wanted. Celebrate, do not second-guess yourself. Besides, as I tell everyone, you can always go back for more, so getting what you want in round one *is* a victory. Here are some positive responses you should prepare for as well:

- "OK, I think I can do this."
- "Sounds good; what do we do next?"
- "It's a stretch right now, but this is important."
- "I never thought I'd be doing something like this, but you convinced me."
- "Yes."

Keep adding to this list in writing, because the last thing you want is to be shocked, stunned, or ill-prepared or have that deer-in-the-headlights look when someone simply says yes to your ask.

Deliver with Confidence

Step two is checked off; now on to step three, deliver with confidence. This may seem beyond obvious, but I have seen many people do all the prep work, then when it comes down to looking the person directly in the eye with strong and convincing body language and tone of voice, they fall apart. Some blurt out the ask so that they can get it over with. Some look down, look away, or look over the person, and the moment of engagement is lost. We covered most of this in this in Chapter 4, under the section "The 10 Essential Characteristics of an Exceptional Asker," so if you need to re-read how you can have the best body language and tone of voice and how you can practice your ask by looking in the mirror and recording your voice, go back to Chapter 4.

I want to add an extra tip for you when you deliver with confidence. What if it is your ask day and you are not in a good mood. Something happened to you in your personal life or you are overloaded with work and it is placing you in a very bad frame of mind. Not every day can be a great day, although we wish it could be. What do you do? How do you get in the right, confident mindset to make your exceptional ask? Well, this has happened to me several times. One time I was so late driving to an appointment that I went over the speed limit in a rural section of New Jersey that just happened to be where many nursing homes were located. A police officer came flying up behind me, pulled me over, and asked me if I knew I was exceeding the speed limit. This was the first time I was ever pulled over, so the officer gave me a warning and I went on my way. That was the day I was doing a $250,000 ask, so I must have been distracted while preparing mentally for the ask. As a result, I lost track of my speed. I was shaken, unfocused, and now so nervous that I could not leave this behind and get a clear focus on my ask.

So I discovered a way to get out of myself and change my frame of mind. I became someone else. That's right; I said to myself, "From this moment on, I am now Candice Bergen," and I visualized how she looked and talked during her comedy series "Murphy Brown." Now, I know I'm dating myself here, but it worked. I loved the way she was strong, funny, compassionate, and in the moment during the shows. She is also the complete opposite of how I look. She is tall, and I'm all of five feet two inches. She has long blonde hair, mine is short. So I stepped out of myself and put myself in the shoes of Candice Bergen, and off I drove to my appointment. It worked. We got the $250,000! Today I visualize

Kate McKinnon the comedian from Saturday Night Live, because I just love her versatile sense of humor and intelligence.

The second tip I have for you when you deliver with confidence is *do it in person*. I've referenced the importance of this several times in this book, but I want to emphasize it here. We know that your ask should make such an impression that it moves a person to action. Let me say this again: Your ask should move a person to action; that is the goal. That impact gets lost or at best diluted when you do it via text, e-mail, instant messaging, snail mail, or the telephone. People cannot see you and they cannot not judge how important this is to you. Even if you do it via Skype, there is still a distance between you and the person you are asking. Yes, there will be instances when it is utterly inconvenient or even impossible to ask in person. This is especially true for international work and for people who work virtually. Also, as mentioned in a previous chapter, younger people may just want you to ask via a text message. But whenever you can, ask in person; as I said before, you have a 75 percent greater chance of getting what you want. Don't underestimate the power of the face-to-face ask.

CLARIFY WHAT YOU THINK YOU HEARD

We are on to step 4, having checked off steps 1 through 3. The first place where the 5-step process can break down is in failing to prepare, as detailed in step 2. The second place it can break down is right here in step 4. By way of illustration, let me show you the importance of this step and how easy it is to skip it. Robert is about to ask a donor he knows very well for a $2.5 million gift for new radiology equipment for a hospital. Robert and the donor have previously discussed the details of the impact of the gift, specifically as to what this new equipment would mean in terms of accuracy and efficiency in patient care as well as the three new technicians that the hospital could hire as a result of this gift. Robert invites the donor to meet with him at the hospital to continue their conversation about the gift opportunity. After a few minutes of catching up, Robert turns to the donor and says, "Thank you for your time today. As you know, we have been discussing the possibility of you and your family making a

$2.5 million gift by the end of this year to support our new radiology equipment and recruiting our new technicians. Have you made a decision, or is there anything we can do at the hospital to help you make that transformational decision?" A great ask. The donor turns to Robert and says, "I do have to think about this." Robert says that's fine, and that he will call the donor in a week or so to follow up.

What went wrong here? At first appearance, absolutely nothing, since it is perfectly normal for a person to need more time to decide on a $2.5 million investment. But here is the missing piece, and we miss it all the time. *Robert has no idea what the donor is thinking about, and therefore he cannot close this gift until he does.* Our minds have the natural tendency to do what I call "fill-in-the-blank work." We start guessing and calculating the exact reason why the person cannot do what we asked, but they have said nothing. Using our example with Robert and the donor, we start guessing that the donor:

1. Thinks $2.5 million is too much money.
2. Hasn't really discussed it with his family yet.
3. Has other charitable commitments that might make this gift too much at this time.
4. Isn't really wild about supporting this project.
5. Perhaps wanted someone from the radiology department to be there.
6. Wanted the ask to be done at his home, not at the hospital.
7. Wanted the whole family to be present during the ask.
8. Expected that he could do the gift mostly through a will.
9. Maybe wanted more details about the estimated number of patients per year that would benefit from this new technology.
10. Wasn't convinced by Robert's delivery of the ask.

These are just 10 reasons, and there could be more. But the problem is that we start racing in our minds about what the donor is thinking, and the *donor has not said a word*. When this happens—and it will—your one and only task is to find out exactly what the person is thinking. Do not leave it to chance or start guessing what it could be. Here is the ask at its best. In this example, the first thing Robert should say when the donor says, "I have to think about it" would be a response such as:

Thank you for your consideration. We are sure this is an important opportunity to consider. To the extent you feel comfortable, can you share with us what you are thinking about? We are here to help.

Thank you for your time. It would be so helpful if we could know what you are thinking about so that we can help you reach this important decision. What is on your mind?

Thank so much for your honesty. We know this is a big decision, and we are here to help you. Together, we know we can reach a decision. Can you let us know what you are thinking about?

These are suggested phrases that will help you get to the bottom of the person's concern so that you are both on the same page. I will reiterate that it will take you much more time to get a definite answer if you do not know what the person is thinking. Once you do, stay with their concern. First, you lead with the thank you because everyone deserves to be thanked for their time and their consideration. Second, you make the invitation to discuss what they are thinking by stating, "To the extent you feel comfortable" or "It would be so helpful." This gives the person the chance to say "No, I'd rather think about this alone," or to let you know exactly what they are thinking. In my 25 years of asking I have never had a person say to me "No, I'd rather think about this alone," so that should give you the confidence to extend the invitation to have the person tell you what they are thinking. Third, when you say "we are here to help you," you let the person know that you are a team. They do not have to resolve this all by themselves.

I have discussed with many people how they felt after they have been asked. Many responded that they felt "put on the spot," "like a floodlight was shining on them," or "pressured to respond right away." This says to me that the ask was blurted out. The asker did not bring the person in close; rather their words, actions, or tone of voice pushed the person away. If you thank the person, ask permission to clarify their response, and end with "We are here to help you;" you keep the person close and agree that "now we can work it out together."

In this example, if the donor says to Robert, "I have other outstanding gift pledges to make, and I don't think I can take this on right now," we know that it is *the timing* that we need to work out. If the donor says to Robert: "I have not made a gift that large; I really feel more comfortable in the $1.5 million range," we know it is *the amount* that we need to address. Whenever someone hears the response "I have to think about it," there is an automatic reaction to think the amount is too high. But remember, that is you the asker making an assumption. In reality the person you asked just said they have to think about it.

Clarifying what you think you heard is such an important step. It applies with any ask. What if you asked a neighbor to help you paint your garage next Saturday and your neighbor says "Gee, I don't know." You could assume that your neighbor:

- Does not want to.
- Is busy next Saturday.
- Doesn't like you enough to give up his day to help you.
- Asked you to do something in the past and you turned him down.
- Has to check with his family to see if there are things he needs to do for them.

All these ideas are swirling in your head, and yet all your neighbor said was "Gee, I don't know." I often say the ask is like a group hug; keep the person you asked close to you. Don't make the ask a tennis match—I speak, you speak, I speak, you speak. Bring the person in close, let them know that you are there to help and that they do not need to make this decision alone. If they want to, fine, but offer to help. The most important thing is to find out what they need in order to reach a decision. In all my years of asking, I have never had someone say to me: "It's private," "I can't tell you," "I don't want to tell you," or "It's none of your business." They will share with you what is on their mind, and once they do that you have successfully clarified the issue. Now, together, you can move forward to reach a decision.

PLAN YOUR NEXT MOVE AT THE ASK

Emma had just launched her own acupuncture business, which she set up in her home. She had been with a small wellness practice but felt that the timing was right for her to branch out on her own. In addition, she lived in a town where there had been major residential and commercial growth, so she saw her opportunity to seize on a new patient base. She was diligently making personal outreach calls and going to local business networking events. Although she met many people who said they would be in contact with her, her business was not taking off, and she was not getting the patient volume she expected. Whenever she would describe the uniqueness of her practice and the person seemed genuinely interested, she would say to them, "Great, give me a call to set up a time to come in for your initial appointment" or "I will call you next week to set up a time."

What went wrong here, and why is Emma not getting any traction for her business? While it appears that Emma was doing step 5, plan your next move at the ask, she wasn't. Saying to someone: "I will call you next week" or "Call me when you want to set up a time to come in" is not planning your next move. Take a look at the difference between saying:

"I will call you next week"

and

"How about if I call you next Tuesday at 10:00 AM?"

Or between

"Call me when you want to set up a time to come in."

And

"I have my first opening Tuesday at 10:00 AM next week. How does that work for you?"

Planning your next move at the ask requires you to be *proactive* and for you to list the suggested *date and time* when you will meet or speak again. That is the way you get your calendar matched with the person you asked. Otherwise it will take you on average two and a half weeks to actually catch the person on the telephone or to get your texts or e-mails returned. I know this from experience! I thought I was doing so well to actually have the person consider my ask that I did not lock down the date and time to speak next. It cost my business dearly because I could have been helping my clients to raise money much more quickly.

When Robert asked for the $2.5 million gift for the radiology department, he made the same mistake. When the donor said "I have to think about it," Robert said, "Fine" and stated that he would call in a week or so. What is a "week or so?" You don't know, and neither does the person you asked. So to satisfy step 5, lock down the date and time to meet or speak next at the ask and watch how quickly your patient and client numbers increase, your timeline to close gifts lessens, and the response from your neighbors comes faster.

Now you see how "The Five- Step Foolproof Method for Any Ask" can work for you in any situation. Remember: it is really important that you do these steps in order and that in step 2 you *write* down all the responses you think you will hear and keep adding to your list. They work, and I am confident they will work for you.

The Ask—It's Two Sentences and a Question

Now that you have my 5-Step Foolproof Method for Any Ask, you can use it to craft your perfect ask. This is one of the biggest jewels of wisdom I can give you. Make your ask *two sentences and a question*. Throughout this book I have been illustrating how important this simple yet highly effective technique can be. The reason why I repeat this technique in every suggested language for your ask is that in my experience people *over-ask the ask*. I know you have experienced that for yourself. A friend asks you to pick up his mail and packages outside his door for two weeks while he is on vacation, and the ask goes like this:

> *Hey, we will be away for the first two weeks in July. Gosh, we can't wait. We are going hiking in the Pacific Northwest. Some of our equipment is still on its way, but it will get here on time. The weather looks terrific, some rain here and there but nothing to worry about. And can you believe my boss gave me such a hard time taking off because we are testing a demo those weeks and I won't be there? Oh yeah, could you pick up my mail and packages those weeks? That would be great. So how about you, vacation plans on the horizon? I remember you said you may be using your frequent flyer miles to go to Spain.*

Sound familiar? Somewhere sandwiched in this lively and exciting conversation is the ask to pick up mail and packages the first two weeks of July. But also there are the comments about the arrival of the equipment, the weather, the boss being reluctant to give the time off, and the question of where the person being asked will vacation. Which part of the conversation should the person being asked address? Now I do not want to steer you away from having a light and easy conversation with your friends, relatives, and neighbors or anyone close to you, but when you want something and need to ask someone for anything, *keep it simple with two sentences and a question*; get your answer and then move on to the weather, the equipment, the boss, and your vacation plans.

Here is how the conversation could go. First, make your opening conversation the way you would normally speak:

> *Hi Carter, how are you? Do you have any vacation plans for the summer?*

Listen to what Carter has to say and then you make your ask:

> *We plan to be away the first two weeks in July, hiking the Pacific Northwest. In the past we have come back to some mail the post office*

forgot to hold, packages by our door, and the mail piled up, which can be a sign that we are not home. Do you think you could pick up any mail or any packages outside our door at that time?

Do you see how this all fits in? With all the preparation work you did with the five steps, now you can glide into the formula for two sentences and a question. Is it magic, no, but it is practical and powerful, oh yes!

If you would like more on the 5-Step Foolproof Method for Any Ask, I highly suggest you read my e-book *Winning Words for Raising Money* (2013, Jossey-Bass). In it I lay out more details on these five steps and particularly how they relate to raising money.

CHAPTER

How to Keep Your Ask on Track

AT THIS POINT, I HAVE SHARED WITH YOU every tip, technique, and occasional trick to use if you have some time to make your ask and if you have more time to do so. I sense by now that you need to know what happens if everything we set into play does not work out as we planned. Well, not every ask goes smoothly, but I'm here to tell you that most asks—yes most—can get back on track. I've had the vantage point to see how anyone can get their ask back on track regardless of the answer. I'm not suggesting you will get what you want every time, but I am stating with certainty that, regardless of the initial response to your ask, you can get it back on track, at least for another consideration. And that, my friends, can be real money in the bank and, even lead to ultimate personal satisfaction.

So in this chapter we are going to discuss whether your ask was really an ask. We'll focus on taking asking U-turns when you hear the word "no" as well as five ways to turn a bad ask into a win. Are you ready? Let's do this!

Was Your Ask Really an ASK?

The first step is to go back with complete honesty and dissect the words you used when you asked. It is one thing to prepare in your head as we saw in Chapter 5, "Prepare the Conversation." That is the polar opposite of writing down the preparation. My suggestion is that when you make your ask, *memorize* as best you can the *exact* words you used. I've done this numerous times; to my surprise I thought I had said one thing and on reflection realized that I really hadn't. Therefore, I'm sharing this with complete candor and total honesty. I thought I was doing a stellar job, but when I went back into my car, the train, or the sidewalk, I realized I had left something out.

It was the end of the year, and I was uncertain whether I had fulfilled my medical-plan deductible. I was certain I had, but I was having some problems with my ear and I also had to see a doctor. When I called to make the appointment, I asked, "Does the doctor take Cigna Insurance?" The receptionist said "Yes" and scheduled my appointment. When I arrived and started filing out the forms, the assistant said that I had not fulfilled my deductible and that although they accepted Cigna Insurance, that was an out-of-network provider and I would have to pay for the full amount for the visit. It would cost me over $300. I thought, "Wait a minute. I did ask this while I set up the appointment." Then when I went over my words "Does the doctor take Cigna Insurance?" it dawned on me: Of course they take it, but would it be accepted as in-network with most of the cost being covered by my insurance? This is how you go over what you think is a stellar ask with all the bases covered to arrive at a humbled moment when you realize you blew it!

This story does have a silver lining, and I did begin this chapter saying that your initial ask can be saved. When I did meet the doctor (and she was delightful), I told her how the "expert on the ask" blew it and did not ask the right information when I set up the appointment. I asked her if there was anything she could do so that I did not have to pay an enormous amount, which I'm sure I would have to once I left her examination. She thought for a minute and then presented me with an ask. It turned out she was thinking about starting a nonprofit and wanted to know her options. She asked me specifically if I thought it was worth her time to start her own nonprofit. After I gave her a bit of advice (and I always advise people first to *collaborate* with existing nonprofits and then see if the nonprofit world is right for you), she gave me a free hearing exam and took $100 off my bill.

I thanked her over and over, and she said that it would have cost her triple in fees and time to get my advice. And the best news was that I just had some extra trickles of water in my ear from swimming and I was fine. The ASK—don't give up when the first go-around does not go your way!

Now we all do second-guessing in our heads, and I often say "It's a crowded house in your head when you keep talking to yourself." I've learned through many, many mistakes how my ask was not what I thought it was.

Here is a list of 20 second-guessing sessions that I have done in my head about my asks:

1. Did I give the exact amount I wanted or did I skip that part?
2. Did I say when I needed it, or did I just ask for it?
3. Did I over-ask the ask by talking too much?
4. Did I give the person enough time to ask questions?
5. Did I stay silent when I asked, or did I keep talking?
6. Did I say why it was important to me or just ask in a general way?
7. Did I explain the impact and what it will do?
8. Did I say why it was important to have this person involved, or did it seem that I could go on to other people and it didn't matter?
9. Did I explain the *match*—how this person's passions would be perfectly matched by this opportunity?
10. Did I listen enough?
11. Did I address their questions?
12. Did they have questions?
13. Do I know what they are thinking about as I leave?
14. Did I read them correctly and gauge their genuine level of interest?
15. Do I know my next steps?
16. Do I know how and when I can get back in touch with them?
17. Do I believe that this is *really* going to happen?
18. Do they still value our relationship after this ask?

19. How do I continue to make them feel special and appreciated regardless of their answer?

20. Why in the world do I do this?

Amazing, yes? Your expert on the ask has these questions constantly going off in her head, and you need to have them too; you really should have these thoughts swirling in your head. If you do, then you are committed to your ask, and that is *exactly* where I want you to be at this point in our journey. Own your ask. When you do, it will stay on track regardless of any initial setback you may experience. *When you ask, there are more beginnings and openings than you think.* Remember that you can always right the ship, at least for one more go-around.

Let's go through some common asks that by now I hope you see are not really the asks you want. They are not really asks, because they will not put the person you ask in the position to answer them the way *you* want. Then I will refine these asks, and you will see the difference. This should harken back to Chapter 5 and step 1, "Know What You Want," with numbers and dates, in the "5-Step Foolproof Method for Any Ask." This is your check on the words you used when you were preparing to ask, including specific dates and times as well as your why—that is, why you want it. Here are some examples.

Was Your Ask Really an ASK:
1. Does the doctor take my insurance? (We know the answer to that one now.)
2. Can I have the car rental weekend package?
3. Can I have more time off?
4. Would you consider increasing your gift from last year?
5. I have this amazing new app. Do you want to invest?
6. You tell us what can you give this year. (Please, please do not use this one!)
7. Three people just committed. Are you in?
8. We would love for you to be more involved. How does that sound to you?

9. Can you do more to help out at home?

10. I'm getting a cosmetic procedure. What do you think?

11. Can you help me?

12. Is my art any good?

13. Can you step up with the children?

14. I'm overloaded with work. Can't someone else do this?

15. I need time for *me*. Don't you understand?

What is drastically wrong with each of these asks? To begin with, none of them is specific; there is no specific amount, no specific purpose, and no specific time stated as to when you want it. Second, most of these asks are really statements disguised as a question. "Can you step up and help with the children?" is really a statement, "Step up and help with the children." "Can you help me?" is really a statement, "Help me." "Is my art any good?" is really a statement, "Tell me my art is good."

Here are the ways you can turn nonspecific asks and statements disguised as asks into real asks. Note that while the ask should consist of two sentences and a question, for these exercises I illustrate a shortened ask:

1. Does the doctor take my insurance?

   I have Cigna insurance, so will all my expenses, including the visit and lab fees, be covered?

2. Can I have the car rental weekend package?

   I saw on your website that I can rent an economy car at this location with a Friday pick up and the following Monday drop-off date for a total of $150 plus taxes. Did I get this right?

3. Can I have more time off?

   According to our company's extended leave policy, I am entitled to an additional three days off and I would like to take them June 15, 16, and 17, so do I have your permission?

4. Would you consider increasing your gift from last year?

You have been an exemplary donor couple, generously giving our organization $25,000 last November. Will you consider at this time increasing your gift to $50,000?

5. I have this amazing new app. Do you want to invest?

We are seeking an investment of $250,000 for a 10 percent share for our new app, which will be really attractive to your customer base, so can we explain how this would work?

6. You tell us what can you give this year? (Please, please do not use this one!)

We have 100 percent participation from our board. Will you consider making a $100,000 commitment so that your investment will be joined with our board's investment?

7. Three people just committed. Are you in?

We just secured three partners for a combined commitment of $15 million. Will you consider being that valued next partner and make a commitment of $5 million?

8. We would love for you to be more involved. How does that sound to you?

As a well-known community leader, will you share your leadership and join our strategic planning committee?

9. Can you do more to help out at home?

Honey, I've been assigned to a project at work this week, and I won't be home until late, so can you take care of dinner all this week?

10. I'm getting a cosmetic procedure. What do you think?

   I know you think I'm crazy, but I am getting Botox injections to remove my forehead wrinkles next Tuesday. Can you come with me and support my decision?

11. Can you help me?

   I need to find a good contractor to paint the interior of my house, and I prefer someone who has worked in our neighborhood, so can you recommend anyone?

12. Is my art any good?

   I just finished these multimedia compositions—can you honestly share with me whether you think the gallery owner would be interested in displaying my art?

13. Can you step up with the children?

   Our babysitter just called and said she is sick and can't watch the kids on Sunday, so what do you say I watch them in the morning and you watch them in the afternoon?

14. I'm overloaded with work. Can't someone else do this?

   I would love to take on this project, and I'm honored that you asked me. Can we talk about how I prioritize this work?

15. I need time for *me*. Don't you understand?

   I feel so overwhelmed and stressed out. Can you understand that I need time alone this weekend?

I hope you now see how simple, small tweaks to *how* you ask make all the difference between a true ask and a weak and unfocused ask. The goal is always to keep it simple and to ensure that the person you are asking has a crystal clear idea what you want, when you want it, and why you want it. Now you are armed and ready to detect when your ask is not really an ask and how you can create that exceptional ask.

ASKING U-TURNS

We started off in Chapter 3 discussing why people don't ask, and the number-one reason was fear of rejection and hearing the word "no." In reality, we know that if you ask, you will often hear the word "no." Just the sound of the word can bring us back to childhood memories of being told we can't do something we really wanted to do. It cuts off our ambitions, our goals, and our dreams. It can make us feel that we are not good enough or what we wanted was not that important. It can shift our values and even make us downright depressed. No wonder people do not want to ask. Hearing no can put them right back in moments like these that bring up negative feelings and regression.

When you hear no to your ask, you probably visualize a steel door slamming in your face, with no room to breathe and nowhere to go. You convince yourself it is over, a done deal, she made up her mind so the best course of action is for you to say thank you and move on. Big mistake! What they did not say but what you think you heard is: "No, this will never happen, not in a million years so please do not ask me ever again." It's true, right? But all they said was no with maybe a line or two why they can't, why they won't, or why they are not interested.

I can share with you that in my more than 25 years of experience I have never had someone say no with a period. They have said no, but there was always a qualifying reason. For example, I have heard:

- "No, I've made all my philanthropic gifts for the year."
- "No, I'm not interested in funding your start-up."
- "No, the type of room you requested is not available."
- "No, I can't volunteer for your run."
- "No, I don't want to pay $100 to go to the reunion."

It will be an extremely rare occasion that you will hear no and that's it, nothing more. That should give you more courage to ask. But let's say you do receive a No. If and when you do, I want you to think of one thing and one thing only:

No now does not necessarily mean *no* later.

This advice is so important that we could add this to the list of asking mantras in Chapter 2. Your only job when you hear no is to *find out why they said no*; everyone has a reason. When you have your facts, you have a course of action. When you have a course of action you are in control. When you are in control, you are in the driver's seat. When you are in the driver's seat, you are moving forward, and nothing can stop your forward motion. You have to know your facts or you can't plan your next move. This harkens back to Chapter 5, "The 5-Step Foolproof Method for Any Ask," steps 4 and 5: "Clarify What You Think You Heard," then "Plan Your Next Move at the Ask." I bet you didn't realize how all of this advice on the ask would tie in, but indeed it does. Here, we need to clarify why the person said no and then plan our next move at the ask.

How do we get to the reason behind the no without coming across as being overly aggressive or sounding too harsh? Whenever you don't know what to say or how to say it, *open-ended questions win the day*. When you get a no response, after you thank the person for their consideration and their time, try asking these questions to get to the facts behind their No response:

- "Can you share with me why you do not want to do this at this time?"
- "Was there something in the way I asked you that is the reason why you said no?"
- "If you could do this over a period of time, would you say yes?"
- "Would you do it if I also brought in two other partners?"
- "Are you concerned that you will not be kept apprised of our progress?"

- "Did I emphasize enough that it is your outside expertise that we need and value the most?"
- "This is so important to us. Can we find a workable solution?"
- "If I follow your advice and it does not work out, will you agree to help me?"
- "Is it the amount or the timing that prevents you from doing it at this time?" (This one is a personal favorite of mine, and you will see why later in the section "Asking Mistakes.")

All these open-ended questions are suggestions for you to use so that you can get to the bottom, the reasoning behind the person's response when it is a no. Pick and choose the ones that best fit your ask and tailor them to your particular situation. Once you have the facts, you can set yourself up for future success. Let's just take the first suggested question, when you would ask, "Can you share with me why you do not want to do this at this time?" Imagine the person says to you, "Well we already have a vendor who provides us the same exact services you offer, and we have no reason to end their contract and go with your company." Terrific, now we know their reason and you can keep this ask alive by saying, "I appreciate that you shared this with us. We promise to stay in contact with you to see whether there are other products we offer that you may need at a later time. Can you share with us when your contract expires with that other company and when your company makes its contract-renewal decisions?" That's how you turn a no into a maybe. Once you know the contract renewal date, you are still in the game to get that company as your partner at a later date. *No now does not necessarily mean no later.* Get the reasoning and go forward!

Let's take the next question you can ask: "Was there something in the way I asked you that is the reason why you said no?" Now not many people would ask this question because it can give the person being asked wide latitude to criticize or critique your ask. But if you make your ask and you read the person's body language as indicating that something is not sitting quite right, this may be the exact question to ask. The person might say: "I wasn't sure whether you wanted me to make this decision or whether you wanted me to ask my boss." Great, now we know the ask was confusing and that we need to be more specific as to who needs to make a decision. If the person says, "I wasn't sure when you needed to know, and I'm asking myself when I could get you that answer," now we know the person needs a deadline.

I use these two examples to illustrate the dangers of making assumptions as to why the person gave you a no response. It is the same danger as we saw in Chapter 5, "The Five-Step Foolproof Method for Any Ask," that come up when we don't clarify what we think we heard. We jump to huge conclusions even though the person has not said anything. We take off in a direction that more often than not confuses the person being asked. *Get to the facts behind the response, and you will be able to get what you want.* It's my legal training that always brings me back to the importance of facts.

Now that you know how to address a no response, let's address when you hear something that sounds like a no. Here are some examples of responses that I have heard that could be interpreted as no's:

- "We just can't do that right now."
- "That's way too much."
- "I'm not interested."
- "When you secure *x* amount come back."
- "You do it first, then I will do it."
- "We have already supported a similar cause."
- "If I do this for you, I have to do it for everyone."
- "I don't have that kind of time to commit."
- "I have to think about it."
- "Why are you asking me?"
- "Can I do this at a later time?"
- "This is all I am authorized to do."
- "I need more information."

- "I have to speak to other people before I can make this decision."
- "Can I have more time?"
- "Who else is investing with you?"
- "Why is this so important to you?"

What is interesting here is that the word no does not appear anywhere in these responses, yet when we hear them, we think they mean no. Why is that? I believe it is because we are so eager to get a yes answer that we jump to the conclusion that anything other than a yes must be a no. I assure you there is a lot between a yes and a no that can get you to that yes. Let me show you how you can convert these seemingly no or negative responses into strong considerations leading up to a yes.

- "We just can't do that right now."

  We are thrilled that you want to partner with us and that timing is your biggest concern. We are here to work with you to get this timing right. Can you share with us whether you have a particular time in mind?

- "That's way too much."

  Yes, this is a large amount; and we do not ask this every day, and we do not we take this size investment lightly. What is important is that this will be meaningful to you and your family. We have some ideas as to how you could do this in installments. May we share them with you?

- "I'm not interested."

  We truly appreciate your honesty, and we would never want you do to something that does not interest you 100 percent. You shared with us before that you wanted to be more active in the community, and we thought joining our community board would match that interest. Would you consider joining one of our committees first and then consider a board position?

- "When you secure *x* amount come back."

  We can appreciate that you wish to see more investment before you make your commitment. We want you to feel solid with your prospective investment. Can you share with us why you want this particular amount to be committed first?

- "You do it first, then I will do it."

  Speaking up at a parent's conference is definitely tough, and we don't want to jeopardize our relationship with the school, but this issue must be addressed. How about if I explain our concerns and what we want, then you can add your concerns. Would that make it more comfortable for you?

- "We have already supported a similar cause."

  That is fantastic and we applaud your philanthropic generosity. We know that you do support that cause but you might not be aware that our programs benefit deserving children with much different needs in drastically different populations. May we explain a bit more?

- "If I do this for you, I have to do it for everyone."

  We know it can feel this way, but we wanted to make sure that you knew how important it is for us to have you and your company to be at our gala. You are our trusted partners, and your presence will be so special and meaningful for us. Can we discuss how we may help you if and when you are approached by other groups?

- "I don't have that kind of time to commit."

  Volunteering for this event can feel like a huge time commitment for sure. With your commitment and that of others, we are sure to have the most successful event. Would you be willing to give us a few hours before the event to help organize the registration?

- "I have to think about it."

  That's fantastic. We are so pleased. We are here to help you reach your decision. To the extent you feel comfortable can you share with us what exactly you are thinking about?

- "Why are you asking me?"

  Conversations with mom are not always easy, and we know that she does listen to you more than anyone. We are here to support you, and we will be there with you when we have the conversation. Why don't we all get together and decide how we are going to present this?

- "Can I do this at a later time?"

  As you know, we do need the seed investment by the end of the year so that we can stick to our production schedule as well as projected revenue. This way, we can attract other investors because we will have your commitment. Would you consider doing half by the end of the year and the other half by March 1?

- "This is all I am authorized to do."

  I appreciate your honesty, and you know how important this paid time off is to me. I have an idea that may be beneficial for both of us. Why don't we have a meeting with the CEO so she can give us a definitive answer on this matter?

- "I need more information."

  Absolutely, we are more than willing to give you whatever additional information you need. We are thrilled that you are so interested in our sports program proposal. Please tell us what you need, how you would like it sent, and the date you need it by?

- "I have to speak to other people before I can make this decision."

  Of course I anticipated that you may want to confer with other family members before you make this important decision. It is always best to have everyone in agreement and to support your decision. Would it be helpful to you and the family if I were present when you have this discussion?

- "Can I have more time?"

  Big decisions like this one require careful thought and planning. We stand ready to help you any way we can. Would it be helpful if we circle back with you in a month so we can revisit this offer?

- "Who else is investing with you?"

  We came to you first because we wanted you to know that having you as our first investor was so important for this project. Your name, reputation in the industry, and most of all your expertise will make it possible for us to attract other investors. Do you have some ideas of whom we can approach after we secure your investment?

- "Why is this so important to you?"

  This is an excellent question and I wish everyone would ask me. My passion is to have everyone feel empowered, ecstatic, and elated with each and every ask they make. In many ways it mirrors your desire to guide, encourage, and strengthen each person you meet to live their best life, doesn't it?

This is how you keep positive when you hear these types of responses that may at first sound like a no or "not likely" answer. Remember, the ask is a conversation not a confrontation, and you need to keep it light and on track by staying positive and focused. Notice *how your response is still two sentences and a question.* This ensures that you keep the ask a positive conversation. Do not give up when you do not hear the words "yes," "OK," "sounds good," "sure I'll do it," "anything for you," or "count me in" when you ask. You crave hearing them, but you can get to them if you stay positive and reinforce their concerns; then you address their concerns by asking a question to learn a bit more. Once you do that, you are totally in sync with helping them to be in the total comfort zone to say yes. Eyes on the prize; you can get to yes using superior listening skills and focus.

ASKING MISTAKES

Mistakes—they are our lessons and our task masters. There will be times when you make a mistake with your ask. Heaven knows, I have made plenty, and I've shared many with you throughout this book. Mistakes are not the end of the world, but they can sabotage you and your ask if you do not recognize them and if you do not learn from them. See if you recognize the ask mistake in the following scenario.

Sales representative Shaun loves his job covering the Southeast Asia region for his company. His immediate supervisor, the sales manager who oversees the four sales representatives in this area, just left the company. Vice President of International Markets, Chloe, promotes Shaun to his boss's job without giving him the "manager" title. She told him that she wants to give him a six-month trial run to see whether he can handle this managerial position before giving him the "manager" title. It is now month seven and Shaun has yet to get the title change. He has been told by Chloe over this period of time that she is pleased with his work, so he translated that to mean the change in title would follow. Since he never formally received a title change, Shaun decides to speak with Chloe.

Shaun: "Chloe, I greatly appreciate your vote of confidence for me to step into the sales manager role several months ago."

Chloe: "That was a good decision for us. Our revenues are up, and our clients seem to be pleased with how things turned out."

Shaun: "That's wonderful to hear. Thank you too for your positive feedback and suggestions you gave me, especially during the first few months. I want to discuss with you something that is very important to me. I love my new role and the fact that I now have management skills in my portfolio. The only thing that is missing is the title change."

Chloe: "I thought that it was taken care of a few weeks ago."

Shaun: "Unfortunately, it hasn't happened. Was there some paperwork I needed to fill out? This may be my oversight, but I assumed when I accepted the new responsibilities that if you were pleased with my work the title change would happen automatically within six months."

Chloe: "Shaun, you should know nothing happens here automatically. Let me look into this."

Shaun: "I greatly appreciate it. It is important for me to share why the title is as important as learning new skills and being promoted. I have found that a more senior title position gives me more leverage, and I have been able to close more sales deals quicker because of my senior rank in the company. My co-workers also need to know that the company promoted me and that this is my new title within our division. Lastly, the title allows me to do my job with continued excellence. I know the company wanted my title to reflect accurately the scope of sales and management that I now do each day."

Chloe: "I hear what you said, and give me a little time to get this resolved."

What jumps out at you about this ask? It was based *entirely on an assumption*. Shaun even admitted it when he said: "This may be my oversight, but I assumed when I accepted the new responsibilities that if you were pleased with my work the title change would happen automatically within six months." Think back to Chapter 3, "Why People Don't Ask," under the section, "The Possibility that the Person Will Give You in Time What You Want without Asking for It." This is a prime example of assuming the person will give it to you. The assumption is that because you deserve it, you don't have to ask for it. Especially in the workplace setting, supervisors are very busy, and one should not assume that they will remember what your new title is supposed to be or when the title change is supposed to take effect.

FIVE WAYS TO TURN A BAD ASK INTO A WIN

1. YOU DIDN'T ASK; YOU ASSUMED IT WOULD HAPPEN. In the scenario with Shaun and Chloe, the mistake was that Shaun assumed. He assumed so much that he waited over six months before asking his supervisor about the title change. Shaun's ask is very salvageable. Despite the fact that he waited too long to ask for the title change, he could have said: "Since you have expressed a number of times that you are extremely satisfied with my work in my new role, I'm asking for my title to be sales manager effective immediately as we agreed when I was promoted" instead of "The only thing that is missing is the title change." What is the difference between those two statements? Think back to Chapter 5, "The Five-Step Fool-proof Method for Any Ask," step 1, "Know Exactly What You Want," with numbers and dates. While this example does not need numbers, *it needs dates*. When Shaun said "effective imme-diately" that is a date. When he said "The only thing missing is the title change" there is no date and now Chloe has no sense of urgency to get Shaun his new title.

What did work well for Shaun in this case is that he explained why it was important to him. This is a perfect illustration of what was highlighted in Chapter 4, in the section "The Three Questions that Come Before Any Ask," Why me? Why now? What will it do? Shaun here laid it all out. He stated that the position gave him more leverage to close more sales deals, that it was important that his colleagues knew he had this managerial position, and that it gave him the satisfaction and recognition that he was doing an excellent job. I firmly believe that in any work situation, you will do well if your supervisor knows your motivation, values, and beliefs that reflect who you are, what matters to you, and how you see your role within the organization. Shaun lays that out nicely here because he touches on how his title is important to his clients; to his ability to close deals more quickly; to his co-workers, who need to know the hierarchy within the organization; and for his own self-worth to know that his job responsibilities match his job title.

2. YOU ASKED WITHOUT INCLUDING OTHER PEOPLE. Believe it or not, this happens more often than we think. I have had firsthand

experience with this when asking for substantial financial support. When I meet anyone and begin to get to know them, asking terrific questions and, yes, being that exceptional listener that I wrote about in Chapter 4, I always ask, "Do you make your own philanthropic decisions, or do you make them with your family, an advisor, or an attorney?" Early in my fundraising career I took the person's word when they answered that question. If the person I was engaging said, "I make my own decisions," I thought to myself OK, when it comes time for the ask I need to have only that person involved. This was a big mistake on my part. Many, many times when I did ask for that substantial philanthropic gift, the person would turn to me and say "Well, you know you really should be asking my wife; she controls our charitable giving" or "I could never make that size gift without my partner being involved." Lately my colleagues share with me that they ask and the response is "my children have to be 100 percent in agreement with this decision."

This also happens quite frequently in the workplace. Considering Shaun in the preceding example, who wants his senior job title. What if Chloe turned to him and said, "Shaun, that is completely out of my hands. You have to go to the senior vice president of international markets and ask him." Shaun would then have to go to the senior vice president and explain everything that was promised to him by Chloe. Better yet, Shaun could bring Chloe into that meeting so she can tell the senior vice president exactly what she promised Shaun and share that his work product merits the new senior job title.

Not involving all the right decision makers during your initial ask is not the end of the world, but I wanted to make sure that you were aware that it happens and not to beat yourself up over it. I did that in the past, so now you don't have to! Yes, it can feel like a colossal mistake, and you can wonder why the person you asked never shared this very important detail with you. After all, if you had known ahead of time that others needed to be involved or that the person who would make the final decision has not thus far been part of any of your interactions, then you would have certainly made it a point to involve that person before you made your ask. Like assuming without asking, this too is very salvageable. If this happens to you, just say honestly and sincerely:

> *Thank you so much for letting me know. Involving your wife and children is terrific because now it is a family philanthropic decision and you all can be proud of the example you set by your generosity. Can we meet with your wife and children early next week?*
>
> *Chloe, I didn't realize that our senior vice president would have to authorize the new job title. I think it would carry great weight if we both met with him together so he can hear from us at the same time how you promoted me, your satisfaction with my work performance, and that the new title would take effect at the end my six months, which was last month. Can I set that meeting up for us?*

You can easily get your ask back on track by recognizing that another person needs to be included before a decision can be reached. Keep calm, keep positive, and be flexible by including other people. At all costs avoid confrontational words and tone such as "Why didn't you share that with me before," or "That just set this whole thing back at my expense." I've heard these said after the ask, and it does nothing but make the person being asked uncomfortable and defensive. Just roll with it, and tell yourself that you are *almost* to a yes.

3. YOU ASKED AT A BAD TIME. Board Member Brad, who is chairing a charity's annual golf tournament, wants to make this event a blockbuster success. At a committee meeting he turns to Development Director Chris and says, "Why don't you ask the community bank to take the lead sponsorship for $25,000. My company has used this bank for years." Chris is thrilled to have this prospect lead and asks Brad for a contact at the bank and to go with him once he gets the meeting. Brad says that he will e-mail him the contact information but it would be better if Chris does it because Brad will be away on business for the few weeks.

Chris makes the call and gets the appointment to see the manager of the bank, Ella. At the meeting Chris shares with Ella that Brad is a fabulous committee chair, totally dedicated to the success of the golf tournament and that Brad is also a proud customer and supporter of her bank. He also told her that Brad would have been at the meeting, but he is away on business. He then tells her that all the proceeds raised will be used further the mission of the charity and will strengthen and empower the community where the bank does business. Just as he is about to tell her the benefits of the $25,000 sponsorship, such as signage throughout the course, a foursome they can select from the bank employees or customers, and a chance to speak at the cocktail reception, Ella says to Chris, "I'd love to help out, but the bank has made all its charitable gifts for the year." That goes over like a lead balloon for Chris. He thanks her for her time and promises to speak with her next year, saying that hopefully the bank will be that $25,000 lead sponsor for next year's golf tournament.

This clearly is the case of making the ask at a bad time. It can happen in many different scenarios. You can ask for a raise, and your boss tells you that the budget has been set for the year and there is no room for raises. You apply for a job, but the job has been filled. You want to take certain weeks off in the summer, but your co-workers already have that time off. You want to have a serious conversation with your significant other or friend, but their family is going through a crisis. You want the company to select you as the executive recruiter, but they have already hired an executive search firm. You ask someone to join your board or to volunteer, but they already serve on another board or volunteer elsewhere. You ask your babysitter to watch your children Friday night, but she is sitting with your neighbor's children.

When this happens, you may not get what you want immediately or at the time you want it, but you will get it the next time or in the very near future if you follow my suggested language. By now I hope you see that any ask mistake, even if it involves bad timing, is salvageable and can be turned into a win pretty quickly. In the scenario with Chris and Ella, instead of Chris saying that he would speak with her next year and hopefully the bank would be a sponsor, he could say:

> *Ella, thank you so much. I'm sure that Brad will be happy to know that his bank wanted to support the golf tournament but could not at this time. We want to make sure we do not miss this partnership opportunity next year. Can you share with me the earliest time we can approach the bank in the new year for a prospective sponsorship for our golf tournament?*

For the other scenarios, the ask can get back on track if you say,

I appreciate that the budget is set for this year. I'd like to revisit my $5,000 salary increase request and need to know when the timing would be best to have this discussion. Can you tell me when we can meet again early in next year before the budget discussions?

I'm so sorry to have missed the opportunity to work with you and your team. I am very serious about my sharing my skills and making myself a prospective new team member. May I call you from time to time to stay in touch with you and to see when there would be a new opening to work with you?

Gosh, I would have loved to have had these weeks off this year. My timing may be off for this year, but I see I need to plan far in advance for next year. Can you tell me when is the earliest time I can put in for vacation time next year?

Julie, I wanted to ask you how to handle the drama of who is being invited to the shore house, but you need to handle this incident involving your son at school. Your family comes first, so let's table this for a while. I will take your lead; when would be a good time for us to talk?

We appreciate that you selected another firm. We would like to stay in touch with you, send you more information about the growth and progress of our company and have the opportunity to convince you that our firm may just be the better fit for what you need. Can you tell us when you will begin your request for proposal process next year?

That association is very lucky to have you as a volunteer. As a colleague, we know your time is precious, and we value everything you can do and share as a volunteer. Can we touch base in a few months so that we make sure we head your list the next time you want to volunteer for an association?

We totally understand that you are not free this Friday. You know, finding reliable babysitters like you is hard. Do you know of anyone you can recommend so we can speak with her and have this person as a backup to you?

Again, you may not get what you want immediately, but if you use some of my suggested comebacks, your ask stays on track and is positioned for quick success in the near future. The real motivation is that if you do not ask the person to reconsider your initial ask at a time when they can make this decision, you may be in the exact same spot—getting a no and leaving empty-handed. If Chris had not asked Ella when the bank would be considering charitable support in the new year, other charities might approach the community bank and Chris would lose out again. If the person making the $5,000 salary increase request had not asked when the budget discussion would take place the following year, that person might not get that raise for two years. If the person who asked a colleague to be a volunteer hadn't obtained the time frame when that volunteer would be available to help their association, the volunteer might offer her services to another association. *Asking at a bad time should never amount to a lost cause or a dead end to your ask.* It does mean that you need to line yourself up to be the first one considered when the time is right for the person you asked.

4. YOU ASKED FOR TOO MUCH. Yes, there are asks that go way over what a person could possibly consider. I believe people do this because they think if they ask for everything, they will at least get something. This typically happens, to my dismay, when asking for money. I can't tell you the number of times someone asks me at a conference, "We really want $250,000 so we should ask for $500,000 right?" I then let out a blood curdling scream and yell "No!" Well actually I scream internally and then tell the person that when you ask, you need to be honest and sincere. Think back on Chapter 4 and all the elements that make up the exceptional asker. None of them said you should exaggerate, overinflate, oversell, or make up an amount that you want.

When you ask for money or for anything, you need to think long and hard about the exact amount you want and the exact details of what you want. Then you ask for it. You do not ever want to be put in the position of the person saying to you, "Why do you need $500,000?" and then you come back with "Well, we really only need $250,000 so we hedged our bets that if we asked for double we would get what we need." You don't want to be in the position of asking for a week off then when your boss challenges you why you need the full week off, you answer, "Well actually I just need three days." You diminish the power of your ask, you come off as totally unprepared, and chances are if you ask that same person for anything in the future, they won't trust you and they won't do it.

Barbara was the head of Internet sales at a very large publishing house, a very senior position. She had been with the publishing house for 14 years, working her way up to this very senior position. While over the years she ignored the invitations from her business school to attend alumni events, a classmate called her and convinced her to go. Reluctantly she went, but she found herself connecting with classmates she had not seen in years and learning about the progress and new programs in her business school. After she had attended several of these events, she came to know the dean of the school very well. The dean asked her whether she would come and speak to the digital entrepreneur class and share her experiences at the publishing house, and she agreed. She had a wonderful experience, and it brought her back to a time when she was in school and open to all new ideas.

Thereafter Barbara thought that it was time that she do something more for her school, because she had been blessed by having received a partial scholarship that made it possible for her to go to college. She and the dean had several meetings to discuss how Barbara could give back. She decided that she wanted to do a large scholarship for women in the business school who concentrated in the school's entrepreneurial track. After much back and forth, the dean convinced her to make a gift of $250,000 that she could pay over five years for a scholarship in her name. Barbara went home and discussed it with her husband, and he agreed to it but wanted to see the proposal in writing before making a formal commitment.

The dean drafted the proposal and made an appointment to meet with both of them in their condo. On the morning of that meeting, the dean decided to check the stock of Barbara's publishing company. The company was doing *very* well and the forecasted revenue projections were solid. He decided that if the company was doing so well and Barbara had been there for quite some time in a senior management role, she could certainly afford more than a $250,000 scholarship. So he took his pen and crossed out $250,000 on the proposal and inserted $500,000 to the proposal.

The dean, with newly edited proposal in hand, met with Barbara and her husband at their condo. After they talked about the weather, upcoming graduation, and summer plans, the dean presented the proposal to Barbara and her husband. Barbara was aghast. She turned to the dean and asked why he had changed the amount. Actually, she asked why he had doubled the amount of the gift. The dean was taken aback that Barbara was angry about the increase in the size of the gift. He was about to explain his rationale when Barbara interrupted him. She reminded him that she agreed to $250,000 and that since he took it upon himself to double the size of the gift, she no longer wanted to give to the business school.

I know you are thinking that this is an egregious example. Who in their right mind would do something like this? Trust me; it happens and unfortunately way too many times. This example had a very bad ending, but it illustrates what can happen when you ask for way too much. Let's turn these facts around and say that when Barbara and the dean were discussing the scholarship, Barbara would not reveal how much she was willing to give. Right then at that moment the dean could have said "Barbara, we have no idea if you can make a gift of this size. In order to achieve what you want to do with your named scholarship it would require a gift of $250,000. Can we talk about how we can make that happen for you?" Now we are in an honest dialogue revealing the cost of the scholarship and Barbara's ability and willingness to make a gift of that size. I like using the phrase, "we have no idea if you can make a gift of this size," which you have seen me use throughout this book, because even if Barbara owned the publishing house and even if she had the assets to do it, would she *want* to make a gift of this size? Having great assets does not automatically translate into the person giving those assets to you or your cause.

I want to make something very clear here about the difference between asking for an amount that is too high *on purpose* and asking for the exact amount you want and giving the person some time to think about it. In the example of Barbara and the dean, the dean really only wanted and needed $250,000 for the scholarship but instead asked for $500,000. That's asking for an amount too high on purpose. If during the discussion with Barbara, the dean had shared with her that it would be a $250,000 gift for what she wanted to accomplish and Barbara had said, "That's a lot of money" or "that sounds high for a scholarship gift," that would be the time for the dean to give Barbara some time to think about it. If after some time Barbara said she could not make a gift that high, the dean would have the choice of either offering her a scholarship at a lower amount with lower benefits or spreading out her gift over more years. If you have the exact amount that you want someone to consider, give them time to think about it. Don't come off the ask amount at the ask if you have thought long and hard about the perfect opportunity with much thought on your part as to the size of the ask.

Asking for too much also happens with work, friends, and family. A co-worker might ask you to proofread a report; you thought it would be only a few pages and it turns out to be well over 150 pages. A friend might ask you to help with a move; you think that it would amount to moving a few boxes for a few hours, and it turns out to be a day-long project involving heavy furniture. A cousin may ask you to watch the dog while he is on vacation, but you didn't know your cousin would be gone for three weeks. If you find yourself in this situation simply say:

I'm sorry, I should have made it clear that the report is a little long—150 pages. I totally understand if you don't have the time to proofread it. It's not due until next Friday; would that give you enough time to give me your feedback?

Moving can be one of the most stressful events, and you always think it will take less time than it does. I understand that giving up a day to do this is way too much and that lifting furniture may be too much. Do you think you could drop by for a few hours and help me out with my boxes?

Boxer would love to see his cousin every day, but I know that a month may be way too inconvenient. I think I can get a neighbor to watch him for one week. Could you do two weeks and let me know which ones, and then I will ask my neighbor?

Asking for too much can generally lend itself to a quick turnaround. Make sure you recognize exactly what it is that feels like too much for the person you are asking, and then explore your options.

5. YOU ASKED BUT LEFT THE BALL IN THEIR COURT. You prepare and prepare and prepare. Your ask is spot on. You feel with every ember that you made an exceptional ask. The person you asked is engaged, smiling, and leaning forward. She says to you, "This sounds terrific, and thanks for thinking of me. Let me get back to you real soon." You shake hands and jump into your car with all the confidence in the world that this will happen.

The next day you leave a thank-you voice mail or text. You call back in two days and send another light message that you were so pleased with your meeting and their enthusiasm and ask when you can meet or talk again to finalize the deal. But you hear nothing back from her. You think to yourself that she is mulling this over, she needs more time. You think to yourself maybe she got pulled away on a high-level project or is out of town for a few days with work. It's probably best to give it some space. Now a week goes by and you have yet to connect. Suddenly you get pulled into a work project or a home responsibility, and Tuesday blends into Friday.

The following Monday when you wanted to pick up the phone again and call, you had no time and now it's Wednesday. Your ask is getting old, very old—in fact, it's two-weeks-plus old. What can you do? So you call again but you get voice mail. So you do it the old fashioned way: You FedEx a package to her office with a fabulous thank-you note and pictures of exactly how it will look when she finally says yes to your ask. Dead silence. So you let time go by because you can't be a pest or that annoying person. Besides you don't want to sound desperate or needy.

What is going on here? What is so wrong? It's plain and simple. You left the ball in her court and it violated step 5 in the 5-Step Foolproof Method for Any Ask; you didn't plan your next move *at the ask!* This scenario can be easily fixed if you say to her:

We are thrilled that you are so excited about our project together. Time is so short; let's make a date right now when I can call you. It's Tuesday, so let me call you Thursday at 10:00 AM on your cell number, OK?

You have to start the follow-up process *at* the ask meeting; otherwise you are in the endless cycle of playing catch-up. Days roll into weeks. Weeks can roll into months. Any ask is important to you, so you want to have her decision as soon as possible. Whether it's business, fundraising, or something dear and sacred for you, time has to be on your side; the only way to get it there is to line up your next move while the ask is being made.

I have had people come up to me and say "Laura, what do I do? I simply can't get an answer," or worse "they won't get back to me." As I peel back the layers of discussions and the timeline at which the ask took place, the big mistakes were:

- They assumed that since the ask went well, the follow-up would be a piece of cake.
- They thought the person would be proactive and get back to them.
- They never thought that the person would be unreachable after the ask.

When you set a time and date to connect at the ask to finalize the answer you at least have a *leverage* point that you can reference in your follow-up. You can say:

Hey Tracey, I am just calling because we agreed we would speak at this time. It's 10:00 AM on Thursday so I will call you in a half-hour; if by chance I do not reach you, I will call again this afternoon and Friday morning. This is too good to let time get between us, wouldn't you agree?

When you plan your next move at the ask you spare yourself a lot of time and effort trying to catch the person at a later time. I share with great confidence and certainty that you have a much better chance of getting the answer to your ask if you plan your next move at the ask. *Don't leave the ball in their court.* Don't leave money on the table when there is no answer. Be proactive at the ask and set up the exact time when you will next connect.

PART

III

What Can You Ask For?

THE ASK for Business—The Stories and the Lessons

NOW COMES THE FUN PART. IN THIS AND the following two chapters we are going to pull together everything I've suggested you do throughout this book. That way you can see exactly how all the tips, tools, steps, and advice come together. I know it is one thing to read through all this practical and highly success-producing material, but it is another thing to see how it actually is applied in daily life. These stories put a spotlight on the essential points I have highlighted throughout the book. They should also provide you with the take-away lessons on how to keep your ask on track no matter what challenges or obstacles arise. So I hope you enjoy these stories, but most important, I hope that you do adapt and apply them immediately to your individual situations and needs. After all, don't you deserve to ask and get everything you want in life?

TOO BIG TO LEARN

A good friend of mine who works at a very large international financial analytic-software and equity-trading company asked me if I would come and speak with their junior sales force team. Although she was not in sales, her department and her responsibilities at the company interacted with the sales department. She shared with me that the junior sales team was doing well, but a competitive product had just come onto the market. Until now, the sales team had had very little competition, so asking for the business and asking for repeat business was not challenging. That game plan changed with the arrival of this competitive product. She knew that my expertise was in asking and thought it would be really beneficial if I could help the team focus their conversations at their sales meetings on the difference between the two products and to be more aggressive in asking for the clients' business.

She spoke with the head of sales who manages the junior sales team, and they agreed that it would be ideal if I could come in on Tuesday very early in the morning when they had their weekly round-up meetings. At these meetings, the team would go around the room and share their successes as well as their difficulty in getting a client to come to the meeting or in closing the sale. This meeting would be different. They wanted me to give them my "10 Tips for Sales Success." Now quite honestly, I never had this type of list, but I'm very good at adapting everything I know about the world of asking and tailoring it to meet whatever the client needs. So after listening to their concerns, I created the 10 tips.

I came in that Tuesday morning and was escorted to a large conference room with huge windows that gave light. I loved it because it can be such a downer when you enter a windowless room. Everyone's energy falls to the floor because there is no light to keep them all awake and alert. Caffeine helps, but there is nothing like light to keep everyone focused and engaged. I sat down, and one by one they entered. Indeed, they were the "junior" sales force. Everyone there was fresh out of college and bursting with energy. I was more than good to go.

We went around the room with light introductions. I always ask people to share with me who they are, how long they have been in their present position, and, most important, what is the one thing they want me to answer before they leave. That helps me to shape the presentation. The last person to introduce himself was the head of sales. Now while he agreed to have me come in and help him with his team, I could sense he was not convinced that what I was about to say would help them. He kept mentioning in his introduction that while I had vast experience with non-profits, this company was far different. I just love when someone in an authoritative role tries to set a tone that is not beneficial to anyone. Blame it on the lawyer in me, but I said to him that if he had not learned one thing new by the time he left this meeting, I would buy him dinner. Well that got his attention and refocused him to give me the benefit of the doubt. It even brought a few sneers from the sales team. I guess they knew something about him that I was about to find out. So I launched into my "10 Tips for Sales Success:"

1. Prioritize the client base.

    a. Use my master chart.

2. Ask the right questions:

    a. What problem do you need our company to solve?

    b. What do you know about our company?

    c. Whom do you know in our company?

    d. What value and efficiency do you see in our product?

    e. When you make an investment with us, as we hope you do, what is most important to you?

    f. Will you be making this important decision, or do we need to speak with others at your company?

    g. What are your expectations if you invest with us?

    h. Thinking ahead, how can we stay in touch with you while you make this important investment decision?

    i. Have you been disappointed with other major product investments, and what can we learn from those experiences?

3. Be a superior listener.

    a. Clients leave clues, and we miss every one of them.

4. Know when to bring in a specialist.

    a. You don't need to know every detail, and doing that sets up the next meeting.

5. Keep it simple and avoid confusion.

    a. Paper and computer screens can be your enemy.

6. ASK for the business.

    a. Why do you want this company as a client?

    b. What will it do for them?

    c. Why do you want their business now?

7. Don't drop them.

   a. The follow-up is where your fortune is made or disappears.

8. Everyone you encounter is a potential client or lead.

   a. In one short sentence share with everyone what you do.

   b. Ask if they are interested learning more.

   c. Ask if they know anyone who cannot function without your products.

   d. Keep it seamless and light, and ask with a sincere smile.

9. Fuel your networks.

   a. Be 90 percent interested in your network contacts, and make your communications only 10 percent about you.

   b. The happier you are, the more attractive you are.

10. Your every move must be organized, structured, and focused.

After I went through these points with stories to highlight each one, the sales team had fabulous questions such as "What if the client doesn't return my call?," "How long do I hang in if they won't make a decision?," and "How do I know which client is a priority, because it's not just based on how much they buy?" In the middle of answering their questions my good friend, the head of sales, interrupts and says, "Laura, we have 1,000-plus clients assigned to each of them. I'm sure this is more than the processes you're talking about."

Clearly he did not know who he was dealing with. So I said to him "I can appreciate your concern, but I've handled 250,000 clients at a time. Would you and the team like to know how I did it while helping the company raise $300,000 million?"

Great ask, right? It stopped him dead in his tracks with a look of disbelief. I told him to go back to my first tip—prioritize your client base using my master chart. He said, "Sure, but what is this chart?" So I shared with him that I had created this chart, which listed my top clients along with my next-best clients. All the

Name	History	Contacts with Dates	ASK with Amount and Date	Follow Up with Dates	Next Steps with Dates

Laura's Master Chart

information is in a database, but the problem is that you have to pull up records one by one to see where your client is in the sales process. It's like fishing; you can pull up only one fish at a time. You can run reports that pull up mounds of data, but it's the activity that has been done and needs to be done that is the most important part in getting the sale. I told him, "If you can run a report that shows only these fields, that's terrific, but if you can't, use the master chart. Then I showed him the chart above.

I warned him that it would appear so simple yet it works, and I shared the details of how his junior sales force could use this master chart. I said that in the first column you list your client's name and the company he represents. So many people list the company and forget the name of the person you need to deal with. The second column I call "history." List the history of sales or specify that this is a first-time client. The point is to list something to stir your recollection of how the company is—or needs to be—an investor. It's not just to import an Excel spreadsheet of business activity.

Next, list the contacts you have made, including dates, and specify what you need to do. Dates are your ultimate friend when it comes to this master chart. It's one thing to say "I have to call my top 15 clients this week," and it's another to visually see that this work has to be done this week. Otherwise, this week rolls into next week, and the next thing you know, you've called 3 of your 15 and it's almost the end of the month.

The fourth column is my personal favorite—ASK. What will you ask for? What is the amount, and *when* will you make the ask? Again, if you do not have the prospective date for your ask, time will roll by as it did with the contacts you needed to make. The fifth column is the follow-up to the ask, with dates. When you will call, drop by, send a text, send additional information, or bring your specialist to the next meeting? Finally, how will you keep the relationship going regardless of the answer? The answer could be that you never get an answer, so what will you do with dates? I reiterated that these would be their top prospective clients, so surely they did not want to drop these top prospects and clients and go on to someone else with just one go-around.

And then it happened. The head of sales turned to his staff and said, "We all have to be using this chart; in fact I'll make the template, tweak it a bit, and we can all put it on our shared drive." Smiling away, he looked extremely satisfied. The junior sales team got their questions answered, and they walked away with a great new and simple tracking tool. I asked him why he liked it so much, given that this is a well-known and highly successful company. He said that they often get lost in all the new technology, and everyone has been spending too much time learning that technology through their computers but not spending the same quality time with clients. It became too transactional. I told him the best piece of advice I could give him and his team was the following: "These are the people making these decisions—or not making these important decisions. They will partner with you if they *know, like, and trust you*. That's it. Keep the emphasis on the relationship, keep it simple, stay organized, and watch your sales team fly."

I ended the meeting asking him if I owed him dinner. He never answered, so I said I would gladly do it because I had learned as much as he and his team had. He said it wasn't necessary but that he would like his next tier of sales folks to have the same training. I never shared with him (though I was dying to tell him) that I had created a similar master chart 20 years ago at a nonprofit.

I didn't tell him, because I feared he would have jumped to the conclusion that what works in nonprofits doesn't necessarily work in business. But one of my quests has been to show how both nonprofits and businesses can work and learn from each other. Mission accomplished!

I hope you can see throughout this story the *organization, structure, and focus* theme that I have emphasized many times. It simply does not matter what kind of ask you make, whether it is for a nonprofit, a business, or yourself. You should keep it structured, especially if there are a lot of people you need to ask. That is why I use the master chart whenever I need to organize a large group of potential investors or donors. It works even if you are planning a social event. The second thing that should tie things together is that, while I called it the "10 Tips for Sales Success" in this story, it is a reiteration and reinforcement of the "10 Characteristics of an Exceptional Asker" presented in Chapter 4. The tools, techniques, and lists I have shared with you in this book can be used for any ask, and I hope this story has emphasized that important piece of advice for you.

PAY ME WHAT I'M WORTH

Kristen loved her job as one of four HVAC mechanical engineers at a family-owned firm. She had been working there for the past two and one-half years with only a slight increase in salary. As a small business, this company did not have a formal policy as to when or how raises were given. Kristen thought it would be good if she asked her boss, Rodger, in mid-October whether she could have an end-of-year raise. She mentioned to Rodger that while she appreciated the vote of confidence he had given her by assigning her some of the top projects, she felt it was time that she received a larger salary increase at the end of the year. Rodger somewhat ignored her conversation and turned the conversation back to how lucky she was to be selected to work on the construction site for the refurbished chapel, the historic local bank, and the gymnasium at the nearby university. While Kristen knew that these were choice projects and that he could have assigned them to her co-workers, she walked away feeling empty from the conversation. Worse, she really didn't know whether Rodger had heard her ask for the raise or whether he was purposely avoiding her.

A few weeks went by, and Kristen had to put in overtime to meet the deadlines for these critical three projects. Working late, she noticed that none of her co-workers were putting in any extra time at work. Thinking about the amount of her overtime work, she felt that this would persuade Rodger to give her a raise. She knocked on his office door and had the following conversation:

Rodger: What's up, Kristen? You look like you have something on your mind.

Kristen: I do, Rodger; thanks for your time. Do you remember that I asked you for a raise a few weeks ago?

Rodger: A raise, hmmm, no I don't remember that at all.

Kristen: Well, I did. I said that while I appreciated being assigned the top three projects, I deserved to have a raise at the end of this year.

Rodger: Kristen, you have always gotten a raise at the end of the year.

Kristen: I know, but this year I want something much larger. After all, I have much more responsibility than my co-workers so I should be compensated for that.

Rodger: Well, you are. I could have given these projects to anyone, and I gave them to you. That's compensation right there. When they are done you have the pride and sense of accomplishment that you did it on behalf of the firm.

Kristen: You may not realize it, but I'm the only one here for the past two weeks putting in a lot of overtime to meet the clients' deadlines for these projects. That should be a very good reason why you would consider giving me a much larger raise than last year.

Rodger: Well Kristen, we all work at our own pace.

Kristen: Rodger, can we at least keep the door open for me to receive a larger raise, and I will come back to you mid-December so we can discuss this again?

Rodger: Sure; my door is always open.

By now Kristen is fuming, frustrated, and fatigued. Each day and night at work she is getting more and more resentful that she is working so hard and it is entirely likely she will not receive a larger salary increase at the end of the year. She resorted to the only way she knows to deal with stress—swim laps. Three times a week after work she went to her local YMCA and swam as many laps as she could to wash away her tension. One night as she was leaving, she ran into her friend Corey. He noticed that she looked distant and not her usual energetic self. After Kristen gave a brief rundown of her frustrations at work, he suggested that she do her research. He told her to find out what other professionals in her field with her experience were making in small firms and in comparable geographic locations. He said that he had been through a similar experience with his boss a few years ago, and while it took a few go-arounds, he got what he wanted and even a promotion in title.

With renewed energy and a clear path, Kristen began her research and started attending career and networking events so that she could get a better handle on the going rate for her line of work and her experience. She realized that despite the extra assignments and overtime, the real focus would be that professionals in her field with her experience, in small firms with compatible geographic areas, should be making on average $15,000 per year more than she was currently receiving. She then took out a piece of paper and wrote down a few things she anticipated Rodger would say when she asked for the raise again. Her list included:

1. If I gave you that much, I'd have to give everyone the same amount.
2. When I hired you, it was at a much higher rate than we could afford, so it's all evening out.
3. We didn't budget for it, so you will have to wait for next year to be considered for that size raise.
4. No one has ever received that amount at one time.
5. We are a small firm, and we can't give out raises that size.
6. I don't receive that kind of raise, just to put it in perspective.
7. Isn't being selected to work on the firm's most prestigious projects worth as much as you're asking?
8. Let's see how the firm does in the next quarter.

9. After these three clients, we don't have any big fish like them in the coming year so things will be tight.

10. Why don't we give you a few extra paid days over the holidays to compensate you for your work?

Not only did she make the list, but she had the answers if and when Rodger gave her one or more of these responses:

1. If I gave you that much, I have to give everyone the same amount.

   That would be the firm's choice. Right now we are only focusing on my request for $15,000. Let's get back to my request, shall we?

2. When I hired you, it was at a much higher rate than we could afford, so it's all evening out.

   I think we both know the reality is that without my work you would not have had the confidence to tell these three top clients that their projects would be completed on deadline. Otherwise, you would have given one or more of these projects to my co-workers. Shall we discuss my $15,000 salary increase for my work and expertise?

3. We didn't budget for it, so you will have to wait for next year to be considered for that size raise.

   I can appreciate the need for a budget; however, when we began this calendar year we did not factor in these three new clients. They have brought the firm a 35 percent increase in revenue over last year. We both agree that I more than deserve this $15,000 increase, which has greatly enriched the reputation of this firm— agreed?

4. No one has ever received that amount at one time.

   There is a first time for everything. Let's set the precedent right now, because having these three clients is an extraordinary and wonderful thing for the firm. Let's focus on the work and comparable compensation, OK?

5. We are a small firm, and we can't give out raises that size.

   It's not the size of the firm that is at issue. What is at issue is compensating me for my work. Would you not agree that the work I have been doing for these three clients has greatly raised the stature and reputation of this firm, locally and regionally?

6. I don't receive that kind of raise, just to put it in perspective.

   Many heads of firms take their compensation increases in other ways. I am not here to speculate how you should be compensated. I am here to discuss my particular situation, so let's get back to this issue, OK?

7. Isn't being selected to work on the firm's most prestigious projects worth as much as you're asking?

   I truly appreciate and I am very flattered that you selected me for these outstanding projects. That's such a vote of confidence. Now that the work is just about completed for all three and on their very strenuous deadlines, let's discuss my $15,000 raise to reward this great work, OK?

8. Let's see how the firm does in the next quarter.

   I have no doubt the firm will continue to attract even more great clients. In fact, I have a lead or two for us. It is important to me that I be rewarded for my present work at the present time, so let's see how we can make that happen right now, OK?

9. After these three clients, we don't have any big fish like them in the coming year so things will be tight.

   We were in the same exact position last year, and we got these three. I have some ideas how we can leverage our work for future clients.

First, let's shore up the detail of my $15,000 raise and then strategize on how we can shape next year, OK?

10. Why don't we give you a few extra paid days over the holidays to compensate you for your work?

A few paid days off would be lovely, but what I'm asking for is a $15,000 salary increase. If you care to give me both, I would be thrilled! But what I want, regardless of whether you give me a few paid days off, and what we need to resolve is my request for a $15,000 salary increase, so let's resolve that first, OK?

Kristen then scheduled a meeting with Rodger for the third week in December and told him the purpose of the meeting would be to circle back on their discussion about her raise. This time she laid out her research, showing him the salary surveys for a person with her experience in comparable geographic markets. Although he did not give a response that squarely fit one of the responses that Kristen had prepared, he did come pretty close when he said: "But we are a small firm, probably much smaller than what you are showing me here." Prepared and ready to go Kristen said, "What really is at stake here is us working together as a team regardless of the size of our firm so that next year we can have three new major projects each quarter. My motivation to achieve this goal is directly tied to the satisfaction in knowing that I went the extra mile for the firm this past quarter and that the firm recognizes and rewards that effort. So can we agree that it would be mutually beneficial to the firm and to me to receive the $15,000 salary increase effective January 1?" Rodger said that he needed a few days to think about it carefully. Kristen, on the spot, set up a meeting for them exactly three days later.

Bingo! Wouldn't you agree that Kristen nailed it? This is such a contrast from where she first started just intimating but not even directly asking Rodger for the raise. So let's look at all the hidden gems we have in this story. First, it illustrates the importance of each step in the 5-Step Foolproof Method for Any Ask presented in Chapter 5. Kristen's first conversation with Rodger never mentioned how much of a raise she wanted or when she wanted it. She also did not do any preparation to anticipate what Rodger would say until she met with him mid-December. While we can't see Kristen's delivery in this written story, I'm sure you will agree that you can hear the difference in her confidence levels when she says,

> *Rodger, can we at least keep the door open for me to receive a larger raise? I will come back to you mid-December so we can discuss this again?*

And

> *What really is really at stake here is us working together as a team regardless of the size of our firm so that next year we can have three new major projects each quarter. My motivation to achieve this goal is directly tied to my satisfaction in knowing that I went the extra mile for the firm this past quarter and that the firm recognizes and rewards that effort. So can we agree that it would be mutually beneficial to the firm and to me to receive the $15,000 salary increase effective January 1?*

She followed step 4 by reiterating what she heard in Rodger's response: that the firm was small, implying that it should not be held to the same compensation standards as other firms. She recognized it and nicely put the emphasis back on her raise. Step 5, "Plan Your Next Move at the Ask," was perfectly executed when she set up the time to meet three days after her ask meeting.

So there you have it—The ASK for Business with many of the concepts and tools I shared with you in previous chapters. Take a minute and think about an ask or the many asks you need to do for business. Run a check-off list to make sure you hit each characteristic to be that exceptional asker. Insert my 5-Step Foolproof Method for Any Ask into your particular situation, and please write down the responses you think you will hear. Then, like Kristen in our story, write what you will say back. It works, and it will work for you!

THE ASK for Philanthropy——The Stories and the Lessons

HAVING WORKED IN THE WONDERFUL field of philanthropy for over 25 years, I could have filled this entire book with my stories about asking people for charitable gifts of every size. But that would not be fair to the readers who want to know about asking for business and for everyday living. Besides, I hope you have found that this book is evenly divided into thirds, with asking advice spread throughout the topics of business, philanthropy, and everyday living.

SO CLOSE, YET SO FAR

One of my very first fundraising jobs when I transitioned from civil litigation to philanthropy was working as a major gifts manager for a hospital in a very rural area. Although the hospital had a strong direct mail program, with patient and supporter mailings and a planned-giving program with supporters placing the hospital in their will or making trust and annuity gifts, it did not have a major-gift program. For this hospital, a donor in the major-gift program was defined as anyone who could make an outright gift of $1,000 or more. They hired me to create the program.

Since this was my very first major-gifts job, I was clueless as to what to do but excited to get to work. I decided to team up with the direct-mail manager at the hospital and, anytime someone made a gift of $500 or more, I asked her to go with me and visit that person. The purpose was to determine whether that person had the capacity and willingness to support the hospital over and above their current direct-mail gift. The operative words here are *over and above*. With any field, whether that be business or philanthropy, everyone has yearly goals. If it appeared that I was *taking* people away from their direct mail gifts, the direct-mail goal would not be met. I thought this was the best win-win solution for the fundraising success of both our departments.

There was a grateful patient, Mary, who had had successful heart surgery at the hospital and whom we visited many times. She loved to share her stories about the doctors, nurses, and radiologists she knew and could recite all the facts about their lives and their families. Every time we saw Mary, she would give us $5,000 without asking. When I went back to my office, my boss would say, "Why don't you visit Mary every day?" "Very funny, "I replied. "It doesn't work that way." Still, it was a point well taken, because if Mary was giving us money without asking, what would she do if we did ask? So I did some research about gifts she had made to other charities, and I had a pretty good idea that Mary could make a gift of $250,000 pledged over five years, bringing her yearly major gift to $50,000 a year. One of the most important elements in preparing to ask a donor for a large gift is finding *the match*. The match is knowing exactly what the donor loves about the organization and matching that with the ideal gift opportunity. For Mary it was easy. She loved what everyone in our cardiology department did for her, so the right match would be to ask her for a $250,000 gift to continue the excellent patient care in our cardiology department.

So I got cracking on writing a persuasive proposal to present to Mary. After I had all the approvals from the hospital to present it to her, I called her to set up a time when I could see her. I shared with her that the purpose of our meeting would be for me to share with her a brand new opportunity to support the hospital. She said that while she would love to see me, she was in the process of selling her house and moving to Naples, Florida. The cold winters were getting to her, and she always knew at some point she would want to retire there. I, of course, understood, and I asked her when she thought she would be in Naples. She said she would there in three months. I shared with her that I had people to see in that area and asked whether she would mind if I saw her in her new home in Naples three months from now. She said that would be wonderful.

I had to make the decision whether to talk to her on the phone about the proposal or to try to see her in person to present her with the proposal before she moved away. My instinct told me that she was consumed with paring down her belongings and moving to a simpler Florida lifestyle, so I decided to wait to present it to her in person in Florida.

Three months went by and I finally had the chance to see Mary in Naples. Her condo was beautiful, right on the bay with tons of sunlight. After we had the chance to catch up with the details of her move and how all her doctors, nurses, and radiologists were doing, I launched into my ask. This was one of the first large asks I ever made, so be gentle with me here!

> *Laura:* Mary, you have been such an amazing supporter of the hospital and the cardiology department. Your gifts have made it possible for so many deserving patients like yourself to receive only the best, state-of-the art patient care. We have a fabulous gift opportunity for you that will only enhance your dedication and generosity with us. May we explain?
>
> *Mary:* Oh dear. (She looked down and withdrawn.)
>
> *Laura:* What's wrong?
>
> *Mary:* The church was here last week. You know the one that I always went to in West Caldwell? They are in a new campaign, and they asked me to make a pledge and I did.
>
> *Laura:* Mary, that's wonderful, and they are as lucky as we are to have you as a loyal supporter. I would still like to share with you this exciting gift opportunity we designed for you. Can I do that now, even if it is something you might consider in the future?
>
> *Mary:* Of course you can, but I don't want you to get your hopes up that I can do both at the same time.

Feeling a bit deflated but sticking to the purpose of why I was meeting with Mary, I shared with her verbally the details of the proposal. I said that I had it all in writing and that I would leave it for her to view at her convenience. At the ask I do not like paper to come between me and the person I am asking. Paper between us makes it difficult if not impossible for me to see their eyes and read body language and gauge their genuine interest in my ask. She said this is exactly what she wanted to support but that it would be impossible for her to support the church and the hospital at the same time. And then I did something I had never done before.

I said to Mary, "May we be your next largest gift?" Honestly, I don't know where that came from, but I had to make sure that after my visit with Mary some other charitable request or business proposition would not get in the way for her to make the gift to the hospital. Additionally, I had to know where the hospital stood on Mary's philanthropic priorities. To my surprise Mary said, "Of course." Then I thought to myself, "Oh great, Laura. What do we do now?" The only thing I did not know was the timing. When would Mary be done with her commitment to the church, and when could ours begin?

So I asked Mary more questions. (Questions are our friends.) I asked her for how many years she would be making her pledge payments to the church, and she said about two years. It was the *about* word that got me thinking and led me to my next question, which I thought of on the spot and had never asked before. I asked Mary "Are you the type of donor who pays a pledge off in even installments? For example, would you be making a payment by December 31 of the first pledge year and December 31 of the second pledge year?" She said "No, I pay it as I go. Sometimes I pay it over a few months, sometimes I make one large payment; it depends on what's happening in the markets." With that response a light bulb switched on. It was entirely possible that Mary could pay this commitment off way before the end of two years. I had to know when she was through paying off that pledge; otherwise another group might ask her for a large gift or large investment and I'd be in the same exact same place waiting again.

My last and final question to Mary was, "Will you let me know when you are finished paying off the church's pledge so that you can begin your most generous gift with us?" She assured me she would. After that visit Mary and I did stay in touch with telephone calls and personalized notes. Exactly one and one-half years later, Mary called me and said she had finished paying the church early and was ready to sign our proposal and begin making her first payment for the cardiology department.

I share this story practically every time I speak, because there are so many lessons I learned from it. It motivated me many years later to create for this book the "10 Characteristics of an

Exceptional Asker" (Chapter 4). I was 100 percent committed to this ask because I knew this would be exactly what Mary would want. I waited to ask in person even though I was dying to do it on the telephone when she first told me she was moving to Naples. I didn't let paper get in the way of the ask so that I could read her body language and gauge her level of interest. I gave it everything I could to be a superior listener even though I got derailed during the ask with just the two words, "Oh dear." I probably did not have positive energy when she told me about her commitment to the church, but I've worked on that over the years. It did reinforce for me that the win is that I made the ask, not the result. Of course, in the end, I got the result I wanted, but I had to exercise a lot of patience and stay vigilant with my follow-up.

This experience also showed me how important and how powerful questions can be in any situation. I've already emphasized the power of questions in Chapter 4. This might have ended quite differently if I had not asked Mary these three critical questions:

1. May we be your next largest gift?
2. Are you the type of donor who pays a pledge off in even installments? For example, would you be making a payment by December 31 of the first pledge year and December 31 of the second pledge year?
3. Will you let me know when you are finished paying off the church's pledge so that you can begin your most generous gift with us?

If I hadn't asked these questions, another group or groups might have met with Mary right after me, and then the hospital would not be her second priority, but rather a third or fourth priority or lower. If I hadn't asked how she makes her pledge payments, I might have *assumed* that she would be done in exactly two years and that she would automatically let us know she was ready to do our pledge. Remember; Chapter 3 brought home the point not to assume someone will give what you want without your having to ask for it. If I had waited another two years or close to that date to revisit my ask, another group or groups might have met with her sooner and we would drop in priority. Finally, being proactive and asking her to let us know when she could start fulfilling our gift pledges ensured that we would be her next priority.

The last tie-in with this story and with the tips in this book is that my mistake was that I didn't prepare enough. I never thought that Mary would say she was already committed and in a significant way to another organization. I did anticipate that she would say:

"That's a big leap from $5,000 to $50,000,"

or

"Let me start with committing $100,000 and if I can do more later I will."

Or even,

"Is this the largest gift to the cardiology department?"

That's about as far as I got on my preparation list. I do believe that sharing this story over these years has shaped how I created the 5-Step Foolproof Method for Any Ask. I did know actually what I wanted in terms of numbers and dates. We wanted $250,000 for the cardiology department, for which she could pay $50,000 a year for five years. I hadn't prepared in writing at least 15 responses she might have given me. I did deliver with confidence, but I admit it got a little shaky when she told me about her commitment to the church. I give myself points for clarifying the results, because all my questions following the ask referenced her church gift. I did plan my next move at the ask, because she agreed and did tell us when she was ready to make her commitment to the hospital. This ended very well for both of us, but it could have had a dead-end result if I had simply walked away and waited exactly two years when her church pledge payments were supposed to end.

I Really Don't Know Anyone Who Could Support Us

I was asked to do a board retreat for a national nonprofit organization's affiliate division. The affiliate was considering a $3 million capital campaign so that they could move to another location and expand their services. They had never done a campaign of any size, so the thought of embarking on a campaign of this magnitude represented a big risk, one that was frightening to many board members. After many conference calls and planning for the day-long retreat, we settled on the agenda and the breakout exercises. One exercise that drew the most conversation was about *identifying new potential supporters*. Board members view this exercise as outing their friends and colleagues.

So I arrived at the home of one of the board members who had graciously agreed to host the retreat. Her home was in an extremely wealthy area of town, and it was filled with magnificent art and antiques. I started the retreat with my "12 Things Every Board Member Can Do to Help with Fundraising." We began with the first one—call or write donors several times a year who have made first-time large gifts or donors who have renewed their gifts, thanking them for their wonderful support. Everyone was smiling, and I could see they thought that my list would be light and helpful with no intrusive activities.

We next moved to my second suggested activity, help *identify new supporters* who may want to know more or be more engaged with us. Everyone's eyes stared down at the floor. People started sitting further back in their seats. Several got up to get more coffee. I asked them why they thought this would be worse than swallowing poison since this was the look on their faces. Many said that they really didn't know anyone. Another said that they had exhausted their friends with requests for other charitable events. Most feared they would be asked in return. If they asked their friends and colleagues to become involved and eventually support the group, then they themselves would be asked to support their friends' charitable causes.

I told them I totally understood, but they had chosen to be on this board and they had an obligation to make sure the organization was fiscally sound. That meant they needed to help with fundraising. They were about to embark on a very ambitious campaign, and they would need to find more people who had been involved before and ask them for large gifts. I walked them through how they could do this. I said that they could say to anyone they are close to:

> *You may know I'm on this board and I am very committed to the work we do and how it empowers and strengthens our community. I'm sure you are asked by a lot of people to get involved with nonprofits. Would you like to know more about what we do? I'd love to share with you a recent experience I just had.*

That's it—just keep it light and simple. The winning formula for board members is to do this seamlessly in their day-to-day lives. Although they listened to what I said, I could see they were not convinced that they could do it or that they wanted to do it. So I thought the best thing to do was to take a break and just let my advice seep in slowly.

I asked our board-member host if I could have a tour of her house. Up until now we were only on the first floor. This mansion had another two floors, and I was very curious to see what the other floors looked like if my host was comfortable with that request. She looked excited to give me the tour, so off we went. We approached the second floor which she said was her "husband's space." The walls were filled with pictures of him and refurbished cars, very expensive and collectible cars with many guy friends all around having a great time. I politely asked whether her husband refurbished cars, and she said "Yes, that is his hobby." I shared with her the love of cars I've had since I was 18 years old. I had a 1968 Mustang, turquoise blue, white leather interior, with dual carburetors and a V-8 engine, and I was in heaven every time I drove it.

So I asked her if her husband knew about her work on this board, her dedication to the organization, and whether we would meet him that evening when the retreat was over? She said he traveled a lot and by that she meant every week. He was rarely home. I said I regretted that we would not meet him and then took a leap of faith and asked her whether she thought any of her husband's friends might want to support the organization as she and her husband had? She thought about it for a bit and said that his friends had done some crowdfunding campaigns for friends and that they might be interested but she didn't know how to approach them. I said that I would come over when her husband was home and together we would share with him the details of our upcoming campaign and find out whether he had any ideas as to which friends might want to be involved. She agreed—as long as I was there, a neutral person, so it would not be all on her. Now we were on our way to engage new people.

Our tour moved to the third floor. We went into a huge room that she called their study. There was a gigantic telescope aimed directly out a window. I asked her whether she looked at the stars at night, and she said sometimes. She invited me to take a look through the telescope, and I did. The first thing I saw was her neighbor's lawn with a number manicured in the grass. I asked her what was this on her neighbor's lawn? She said that her neighbor Tony, a famous basketball player, liked to display his number on his lawn. I thought to myself, "You really don't know anyone who could help us? First we have your husband's friends who have the hobby of refurbishing collectible cars and doing crowdfunding, and now we have a famous basketball player across the street."

Treading on this ever so gently, I asked her whether she knew him or his family? She said that he and his wife go to social events now and then. I turned to her and asked, "Do you ever have both of them over?" She said, "Only in the summer once the basketball season is over, because it is easier to have them both over for dinner at that time." I thought to myself, "Now what do I do to put this all together?" So I asked her whether this summer, which was only a few months away, she could invite them over and I would script her how she and hopefully her husband could let them know about her board experience and the upcoming campaign and see how they would respond? She at first looked hesitant but then said she would try. She wanted to be sure that whatever she said would not turn off her neighbors. I told her she had my word and that I would do everything I could to make that get-together as light and engaging as possible.

Now that my house tour was over, my last ask of her was whether she could share with the board members downstairs everything we had accomplished. She said that we had not accomplished a thing other than sharing stories about her husband and her neighbor. I said that we had accomplished a great deal, because now we have these possibilities:

- Her husband being more informed.
- Her husband potentially opening doors to his friends.
- His friends being more involved.
- His friends being possible supporters.
- Their neighbors being more informed and becoming potential supporters.

The best part was that even if none of this came to realization, she now knew how to think outside of her comfort zone and suggest family and friends who might—just might—be interested in the work of the organization. She did have new people she could speak to and, with the right approach, no one would be offended or become uncomfortable.

I share this story because no one likes to out a family member, friend, or colleague. But when you see how you can think of people in your everyday life who are right in front of you every day, they may be the people who want to be involved in what you do. Think back to Chapter 4 and reasons, why people don't want to ask. This scenario fits right within the many reasons why many people do not want to ask their family, friends, and colleagues to get involved from the beginning. They jump at the fear that they will have to ask for money right away, when the first step is to just think about who might be interested and how to share experiences. Done the right way, as this story shows, no one will be offended. In fact, many are flattered you thought enough about them to involve them with your passion.

Following this experience I've come to use an additional way to encourage people to think about close friends, colleagues, and relatives they know in their day-to-day lives who might want to become involved with the charitable work you do. Ask them to keep a "people journal." Each day they can write down who they have spoken to, how well they know the person, and where they met. During the course of the day, we interact with so many people, and many times we have stronger relationships than we might realize. For example, someone could go to their gym several mornings a week, get coffee or breakfast at the same place, park their car in the same parking garage, speak with friends or family during the day, go to book club or after-work meetings, take an online class, volunteer for a community project, or watch their son's or daughter's lacrosse game on the weekends. The point is that we often don't think of people who are right in front of us every day whom we already know and who like and trust us. We have the tendency to qualify people very quickly. We think to ourselves, "This group of people I can approach but that group of people I really don't want to approach." In reality, everyone you encounter has the potential to help you so why would you weed some in and weed others out? We are back to the making-assumptions stage, which we now know will not help you in the least. Just by using the easy and simple two-sentences-and-a-question ask, you can expand your prospective base of supporters who might just be your friends, colleagues, and family.

I hope these experiences motivate and encourage you to invite the people that you know and interact with to get to know your philanthropic work so that in time you can ask for a philanthropic gift. A caveat that I must mention is not to let the gift size determine whether you need to apply what you have learned here. Many people may feel that what I have detailed in this chapter applies only to "those big philanthropic gifts." I have done just as much work for a $100 gift as I have for a $100,000 or a $1 million gift. Sometimes the smaller ones are the harder ones and require more work! There are over 1.4 million registered charities in the United States alone. They need great folks like you to be engaged and help them raise money. Now you know how to engage them, to be yourself, and let this be a natural and easy process. Hold on to the organizational, structural, and focusing techniques that you now know how to apply and watch your fundraising soar!

THE ASK for Everyday Living—The Stories and the Lessons

I'VE BEEN DYING TO GET TO THIS CHAPTER and terrified at the same time. How does one condense "asks for everyday living" into one or two examples? I ask—and it's a good ask—that you take the examples that I share with you and extrapolate them into any area of everyday living, whether it be relationships, health, finance, beauty, travel and leisure, retirement, spirituality, diet, exercise, fun, or creativity. I will illustrate how important it is to apply what you have right here at your fingertips in this book to any situation in your life. It may seem more logical or more necessary for you to apply The ASK in business or philanthropy, because those areas are most structured and they cry out for asking and getting concrete things such as money.

But when it comes to our everyday lives, the reward for your ask may be money, but more often it is *personal satisfaction*. It's satisfaction knowing your significant other still loves you when you need more space, your roommate will clean the apartment more regularly, your doctor will give you alternatives to surgery, your son will take your advice and accept the job, your wife will understand that it's time for you to retire, your friends will understand when you skip brunch to attend a prayer group, and your brother will understand that you can't watch your niece because it's the same night as your voice lesson. While I could have selected many examples to illustrate how The ASK works in our daily lives, the first example I share is a personal and humorous example from my life on the road, trying to get a hotel room that I wanted and needed (again). The second is the delicate discussion about money and love. What do you do when you need to ask the one you love either to spend more or spend less?

Is This a Room, or Is This a Closet?

Travel can be wonderful and relaxing, but when you do it for work and you travel a lot, it can be tedious, frustrating, and anxiety provoking. Whether you travel for work or travel as a getaway, I think you will agree that having the ideal hotel room, suite, villa, cabin, or apartment when you are away from home is important. In fact, I would guess that it is among your top priorities when you travel. Have you ever made a hotel arrangement and specifically asked for the ocean or waterfront view and when you arrive find that your room is facing the parking lot? It's frustrating, and you have choices: You can complain, scream at the front desk, or listen to your travel companion who says, "It's not that bad and we won't be in the room that long." Alternatively, you could ask for the room you want that will make you happy and satisfied. The ASK to the rescue!

I was invited to speak at a very large conference in San Antonio. People from dozens of foreign countries were coming, and the crowd was expected to be in the thousands. The topic that I was speaking about was a brand-new concept I had created called "The Five Askers." I had read Gary Chapman's book *The 5 Love Languages* and later on I saw him on an interview with Oprah. I got to thinking, if Gary can put the huge topic of love into five personality traits, I can certainly put the huge topic of asking into five personality traits. So I created "The Five Askers," and this conference was the first occasion I was going to reveal it. (Stay tuned: *The Five Askers* will be my next book—shameless advertisement!)

With a conference this size I knew that most of the hotels would be filled to the maximum. I made my reservation well ahead of time and put in the special request section in the reservation form, as I always do, "Please give me a room away from elevators and ice and vending machines, one on a high floor with no traffic or parking-lot view." I was an affinity member with this hotel in San Antonio, having racked up points for more than eight years, so I felt very sure that that they would honor my requests in my reservation. I arrived in San Antonio and headed directly to the hotel. The lobby area was packed, and there was a very long line at the registration desk. I finally got to the registration desk and

Mason (I always make sure I get the name of the person checking me in) was very quick to greet me; he confirmed my two-night stay and gave me the room key. I managed to squeeze in that I hoped the room was the type I requested because I was a speaker at this conference and I needed it to be quiet so I could concentrate. He barely looked up at me but did manage to say that the hotel was completely sold out. I think they do this so that you will be gratified that you have a room at all.

So up I go on the elevator and then head my way to my room, number 1501. From the minute I got off the elevator I knew this wasn't going to go well. The room was directly next to the elevator and adjacent to that fabulous ice machine that sounds like a constant pile driver. With my hand firmly gripping my luggage, I opened the door and the room was size of a closet—no joke! You could stretch your arms out and touch both walls. By now I was frustrated, but I didn't know what to do. On the one hand, I had made a request ahead of time but it had been blatantly ignored. On the other hand, the hotel was sold out. Still, I could not stop thinking that since I'm a female and I stand a statuesque 5' 2" they thought this would be fine with me. My last thought was that they would never do this to a guy, and that pushed me over. Then I thought, "Wait a minute. I need to go down there and ask, the right way, for a better room." You'd think the "ask" part would have come as my first thought, but sometimes frustration gets the better part of your clear thinking.

So I went back down to the reception area and stood in line again. I could have gone directly to Mason and pushed my way past people, but I thought that would be rude and they would have no idea why I was pushing my way to the front of the line. I finally got my turn with Mason at the desk and this is how it went:

> *Laura:* Mason, I know you did your very best to get me a room while you are sold out and I so appreciate it. The room you gave is really, really small, by the elevator and ice machine, and I need a better room because I'm the keynote speaker at this conference and I've got to concentrate. Can we take a look at your room chart together and see what options we have to get me a better room?

> *Mason:* Ms. Fredricks, I'm so sorry! Let me get the room chart and
> see what's available. It will be a long shot, but I will try to help
> you.

With that, Mason pulled out a laminated room layout chart. I was stunned. I thought he would dive into his computer, punch on a few keys, and say to me that all the rooms were filled. Instead he carefully looked it over and said that he had a room way at the end of the hallway that might work. I thought anything would be better than what I had, so I thanked him and took my new room key. I looked at the tiny billfold card that contained my new key and it had number 1536. I said to myself, "This will be good; at least I'm away from the elevator and the pile-driver ice machine."

On coming off the elevator, I proceeded to walk down a long hall on the 15th floor until I came to room 1536. It was the last room on the floor, and I thought to myself "This could be great." I opened the door, and there was a palatial room. It had a large sitting area with a couch and a modern desk, a bathroom with double sinks, and a view overlooking the River Walk in San Antonio. The bonus was that I could open my sliding glass door and walk out onto my very own private deck, complete with a table and six chairs. Sweet! I thought to myself, "This ask stuff really works."

Later that afternoon I went out and got Mason a cappuccino and brought it directly to him at the reservation desk. I thanked him profusely for what he had done for me. He smiled and said it was his pleasure to help me and that he had done so "because I asked."

I shared this story with you because The ASK does work when you need something that is important to you. I could have gone back to Mason the first go-around and screamed at him or pulled a fit when I got my closet room. You've seen people do this, and it is ugly and pointless. I told Mason the why—why I needed a room that was better than the one he gave me. This gets back to Chapter 4 and the three questions that come to answer before any ask: Why me? Why now? What will it do? I was a featured speaker at a very large conference, and it was a big deal that the room be quiet and comfortable. I needed it now, because if I had waited any longer, any possible available room would be gone. Once I got a good room, I would be able to concentrate and focus on delivering an amazing and engaging session that I hoped would empower the people in the audience to identify the type of asker they currently are and learn the traits they needed to adapt to become the asker they wanted to be. Don't ever settle for an inferior room. Your comfort matters most, so just ask for it!

THE SPENDER VERSUS THE SAVER

In the ideal world couples would share the same spending and saving habits. They would share information about their spending habits, income, savings, investments, debts, and most important *what they do or want to do with their money*. In reality, it rarely happens that couples are totally in sync with saving and spending habits. The worst part is that they rarely ask each other about it and instead just use their money in the ways that make them happy and secure. A recent Experian Credit Score Newlywed Survey Report 2016 showed that newlyweds spend on average $808 before sharing that information with each other.[1] Men spend $1,259 and women spend $383 before sharing these spending sprees with each other. When this happens it usually triggers the money blockers we discussed in Chapter 1 as well as the reasons why people don't ask in Chapter 3. Here is a perfect illustration of what can drive a damaging wedge between couples who don't ask each other about money when they need to get in sync with their views on money. We know from Chapter 1 that knowing your views on money and then sharing those views is the place to begin when you want to be *money balanced*.

Chung and Ava, both in their early 20's, met on Tinder. They hated dating apps, but their friends encouraged them to give it a try. After a few rocky dates, Chung was about to give the whole thing up when he swiped the app on his phone and met Ava—and she was stunning! They dated for a year, and Chung knew this was getting serious. They both had plans to attend graduate school and didn't know how their relationship would fit in with these plans. He wanted to be an attorney, and she wanted to be a physical and

---

[1] https://www.experianplc.com/media/news/2016/newlywed-survey-2016

occupational therapist. While they were dating, Chung would propose doing modest things like local concerts, bicycle rides at the county park, dinner with friends and family, and a summer vacation at a beach house. Ava was totally fine with that and never asked or said that she wanted to do things that were more extravagant, such as going to see their relatives in China, vacationing in Paris, or eating in five-star restaurants.

He finally asked her to marry him and she said yes, but they had to talk about how this would fit in with their plans to attend graduate school. Chung said he would hold off with his plans to attend law school because he was doing very well as a paralegal in a medium-sized intellectual property law firm. Ava said she would keep her digital designer job until after they were married and then begin graduate school. Both agreed that they should save up their money so they could have the wedding of their dreams.

As they began to plan for their wedding, it was clear they had very different ideas of what a "wedding of their dreams" would be. Ava needed—and she used the word "needed"—to have 200 people, which would include all her relatives, friends, and business contacts. Chung had only 50 people, counting relatives, friends and business contacts and assumed Ava would have to be more selective as to who she would invite. To him, 250 people was way too many, and of course it would cost a fortune. After much back and forth, Chung found a way to make it happen with 250 people by cutting back on some of their original plans. Instead of having a formal dinner they would have an elaborate cocktail reception, and since they both just had a best man and a maid of honor in the wedding party, they eliminated the rehearsal dinner.

Four months later Ava was pregnant. While they were both thrilled to start a new family, Chung felt the pressure of now taking on a wedding, a new wife and a child, and Ava's graduate school. Chung was the youngest child in his family. When his mother died when he five years old, his father raised him to always make sure that his three sisters were taken care of. He had an ingrained caretaker sense that he as the man needed to take care of the women in his life, who were his sisters at that time. Now it was his obligation to take care of Ava. Since Ava was pregnant, she had told Chung that she no longer wanted to work until after the wedding and after the baby was born. She would go to graduate school part time after she had the baby. Relieved not to have a graduate school payment, Chung was still faced with one income not two, a wedding, and a new child.

To cover the new expenses Chung started working extra hours at the law firm. To save even more money, Ava moved into Chung's apartment so they could save on her rent. Since Ava was not working at the time, she did not feel the need to help Chung with the rent. To add more stress to Chung's finances Ava was buying things she "needed" for the baby and herself. Chung's resentment started to build, but instead of talking to Ava about the pressure he was feeling about money he kept it to himself. He justified that once the baby was born and Ava was strong enough to go back to work, everything would even out. Also Ava reminded Chung that since she was an only child, her family would naturally give them a very large wedding present and that should help with the finances in their first year of marriage and the new baby.

They had the wedding, and all 250 people came. Even though Ava's family knew that it would only be an extensive cocktail hour, not a dinner, they voiced their opinion several times that there was not enough food for the guests and they were embarrassed. Chung felt upset, because he was the one who suggested they change the wedding from a dinner to a cocktail reception. Towards the end of the evening, Ava's parents approached Chung and gave him a large rectangular beautifully wrapped box and said "Congratulations to the both of you, and Chung welcome to the family." Chung put the present in a very special place because he knew it would be quite valuable.

The next day while they both were recovering from all the smiles, pictures, and dances, they began opening their wedding cards and presents. Chung told Ava that her parents had given them this present and she insisted that he open it. He opened the present and it contained a few gold necklaces, a bracelet, and a ring. Ava was thrilled because these were precious antique heirlooms handed down from her great-grandmother. Chung was stunned. He anticipated it would be cash. He closed the box and walked out of the room; the arguments began, and they were all about money. How were they to pay for everything on one salary?

Why didn't she work longer? How could either one of them go to graduate school knowing they will be straddled with six-figure loans while starting a new family? How could they ever save for a house? Why weren't her parent's doing more to help?

This story could have had a much happier ending if both Chung and Ava had sat down and asked each other more questions instead of keeping it inside or making assumptions. On the surface, this story could be about two young people who should have had a few conversations to put them on the same page about their lives. But I chose the story to show you that are so many factors that go *unaddressed every day*. If we just applied some of our ask techniques it would enhance the quality of our lives tremendously. In just this one story there are deep-seated, value-laden issues:

- **Dating:** How is money spent when you first start dating, and does that change as the relationship progresses?
- **Professional achievements:** Are they fulfilled, postponed, or never realized?
- **Expenses:** Are they shared or put on one person during the relationship?
- **Balance:** Is it fair for one person to work and pay more of the bills while the other stays home?
- **Salary:** When one person has a larger salary, should that person pay more for everything?
- **Shopping:** Should couples agree on every purchase made during the relationship?
- **Weddings:** How do you ask someone to cut the guest list and scale back on the wedding plans?
- **Parents:** Is it right to expect that they will give the couple a fabulous monetary gift at the wedding, or would that make them feel dependent?
- **Care-giving:** Can a person find a middle ground and not jeopardize the relationship by an overly developed sense of responsibility?

- **Expectations:** Can you confuse optimism with expectations when you expect too much and get too little?

And did you think this was just a story with a couple that could not communicate? Unfortunately these hidden issues can and do sabotage our daily lives because they go unaddressed. So let's apply some of the ask techniques you now have at your fingertips and see how we can put The ASK into these everyday situations. Here are some of the things Chung and Ava could have asked each other at the right time before resentment and expectations created a wedge in their relationship:

Dating: *"Ava, I love to do these fun and simple things with you. It gives us the time to spend with each other and do the things we both love. Is there anything you want to do that we are not doing?"*

Professional achievements: *"Chung, it is really important that both of us pursue our graduate education. We both need to work full time, and I don't want too many years to slip away before we can attend. Why don't we consider schools that have a strong online program to at least get us going?"*

Expenses: *"Ava, we need to talk about our living expenses. Right now we have bills for the rent, utilities, insurance, food, cell phones, and credit cards. Why don't we agree to split all the bills evenly except for our separate credit card bills that we use to buy things just for ourselves?"*

Balance: *"Chung, I'm feeling guilty that you have to pay for so many things while I am out of work. I thought a lot about it, and this is what I'd like to do. How about I make your life easier by shopping, cooking, cleaning, and preparing all our meals so that you don't have to worry about any of that?"*

Salary: *"Ava, I hope you don't mind but I've been thinking that it's not really fair for you to be paying for all the things that you do while I at this time have a higher-paying job. During our relationship I'm sure that we will be going back and forth with different jobs at different salaries. For now while I have this job, why don't I pay the car payments and the insurance?"*

Shopping: *"Ava, I can see how excited you are with the new baby and all the things we need. I'd like to be a part of the process when you buy things, because then I feel like we are doing this together. Can* *we agree that when it comes to buying things for the baby we sit down and decide together?"*

Weddings: *"Chung, I know that I have so many more people to invite to our wedding than you and I want to be fair to you and at the same time not disappoint my family, friends, and colleagues. I need your help here. What is the maximum amount of people we should have at our wedding?"*

Parents: *"Ava, I don't want your parents to think that they have to go out of their way and do something extravagant for us for the wedding. In fact, that would make me feel very uncomfortable. What can we say to them to let them know our feelings about this in a way that doesn't come off as presumptuous?"*

Care-giving: *"Chung, I know and you have shared how hard it is for you to let go when your instincts tell you to dive in and take care of someone. Honestly, I'm fine and the baby is fine. What would make me happiest is your focusing more on you. Can I help you in any way to do that, maybe in small steps?"*

Expectations: *"Ava, I know it's wrong of me to have expected that your parents were going to give us money for the wedding. Their gift is extremely thoughtful, and it means a great deal to you, which is most important. Just give me a little time to myself to deal with this, because I don't want to come off as ungrateful or just focused on money, OK?"*

It just takes a little time and a little effort to see how your asks can explore each other's feelings and to resolve those personal and important decisions you have in all your relationships and your everyday life. In addition, this story not only highlights 10 very common areas that we deal with from time to time, it also puts the spotlight on everything we covered in Chapter 1, the importance of what money means to you and what money means to the person you are involved with. On the one hand, Chung has the over-developed sense of responsibility to work and save and watch every expense. Ava, on the other hand, seems as happy as possible staying at home, not working, not bringing in a salary, and spending money on the baby and herself. Chung's money blocker is that if he just hangs in until after the baby is born, everything will even out. That money blocker prevents him from addressing his resentment that he is working longer and harder and that he has to cut back wedding expenses because they can't afford the wedding of Ava and her parents' dreams.

This story brings to light that you have to get straight with your own views on money as well as the views of any other person that you are dealing with, *especially* if that person is someone you love. If you don't have those conversations and ask each other the right questions, one issue rolls into the next, and before you know it days, months, and even years go by with both of you making decisions that infuriate the other. The tips and suggested asks given throughout this book will provide you the freedom, guidance, and confidence to make sure you are in sync with your views on money, especially if they concern someone you care about deeply.

The Hardest Asks You Will Ever Make

WHEN YOU SEE THE TITLE OF THIS chapter, what comes to mind? Asking for the largest amount of money you have ever asked for in your life? Asking for a huge favor when you anticipate that the person you ask will have to go way out of his or her way to help you? Asking someone to lend you money when you think they will judge your ability to manage your finances? Asking your adult child to move out and be more responsible? Asking your father to accept that your mom needs nursing care that he cannot provide? Asking your spouse or partner to work less so that you can have more together time? Asking your friends to accept that you chose to have cosmetic surgery so that you can feel young and attractive? Asking your new girlfriend to spend less time with her friends and family and more time with you? Asking your boyfriend to attend religious services with you so that you can grow as a couple? Asking your boss for a raise and a new job title when you have never asked for either previously? Asking your relatives to stop talking about politics whenever you get together?

While all of these are incredibly hard asks to make, and I do not take for granted the anxiety they can cause, it is my firm belief that the *hardest asks you will ever make are the asks you make of yourself*. It takes a lot of courage, strength, fortitude, determination, and desire to put yourself first, above any other person or any situation, and ask yourself for something that you know in your heart you want and deserve.

The Asks You Need to Make for Yourself

Take a minute and just think about the following asks, and see if you have ever thought about asking yourself for these things or have actually taken the time and made the ask of yourself:

- To be forgiven
- To have more strength
- To let go
- To have more patience
- To be more accepting
- To be a better listener
- To be guided
- To be liked
- To be loved
- To be heard
- To have faith
- To take the time to pray
- To have more fun
- To be more creative
- To be taken more seriously
- To get help
- To nurture your soul
- To get more exercise
- To get more sleep
- To eat less
- To eat healthier
- To be on time
- To be recognized
- To take better care of yourself
- To put yourself first

I could keep adding to this list, but I think you now see the importance and impact of the asks you make of and for yourself.

Every day we have these ask conversations with ourselves about what we want and then make the decision as to what we will do. The problem for all of us is that we think about these asks, but then we justify them away. Here are the ways we justify *not* making the ask of ourselves:

- Time will heal all. I really don't have to ask for an apology.
- I'll get through this. I always do.
- I'm really hurt but too angry to do anything.
- I'm a patient person. I will wait it out.
- I'm always the one who gives in. Let someone else do it this time.
- If they just listen to what I have to say, we can resolve this.
- My instincts are always right. I don't need any advice.
- If I go out of my way a bit more, she will like me.
- I know he loves me. I don't need to hear it all the time.
- I know they are listening. They just don't admit it.
- I attend religious services. That's a demonstration of my faith.
- I'll take the time to pray each morning, starting next week.
- I'm too busy to figure out how to have more fun.
- I'm creative in my work; that's enough.
- It is not that important that they don't take me seriously.
- I'm fine on my own; I don't need anyone's help.
- I'm a spiritual person; people just don't see it.
- I'll try walking more each week. That's good exercise.
- Five hours a night of sleep is more than most people get.
- If I skip breakfast I'll lose weight.
- Next time I go to the grocery store, I'll buy nothing but organic products.
- Everyone shows up late for work; it's no big deal.
- There are so many other people who do what I do. I understand why they didn't select me.

- When I get home I'll deal with my migraine. For now I just have to deal with the pain.
- My family comes first, then I can take care of me.

So the question becomes, are the asks you need to make for yourself any different from the asks you make of other people? To me, all the tips, techniques, steps, and rules apply, but *it is the soul-searching preparation that takes on a whole new meaning.* There is a lot of soul-searching you must do when you get to the point of asking yourself "Can I do this? Can I ask for forgiveness? Can I ask for help? Can I ask and not be judged? Can I ask for permission?" Just this last example would involve permission to:

- Do what you have not done.
- Define success for you and you alone.
- Say no.
- Say yes.
- Take time for yourself.
- Create massive change.
- Take a big risk.
- Change what is not working.
- Congratulate yourself.
- Be wrong.
- Be right.
- Be upset.
- Be forgiving.

In a *New York Times* editorial, columnist Thomas Friedman wrote, "One reason for our resilience as a nation is that Americans have always had the capacity to forgive one another, when the asking is sincere."[1]

On that note, let's take the example of the ask to be forgiven and apply the three questions from Chapter 4 and the "5-Step

---

[1] Thomas L. Friedman, *New York Times* editorial, November 9, 2016, "We're near the Breaking Point."

Foolproof Method for Any Ask" from Chapter 5. Perhaps you have been in a situation where you hurt someone very close to you, maybe a dear family member or a lifelong friend. Maybe they wanted you to come with them to a doctor's appointment or to an event, and you said you were busy. It turns out you really did not want to go and they found out you really were available but made up an excuse. Or you confronted someone close to you, and the conversation got out of hand and you wound up saying things that were extremely derogatory and hurtful. It could even be that your neighbor, who you have known for years, constantly shovels his snow in front of your driveway. Instead of calmly asking him to stop, you angrily shout at him, catching him completely off guard.

The three questions can easily be applied when asking for forgiveness. First, why you? Well, you are the one that caused the disagreement or the argument, so you are the one that needs to do the ask. I do not advise sending someone else to do the ask. It rarely goes well. Can you imagine sending your daughter, a partner, or an uncle to say to your friend, "I'm sorry she did not go to the doctor's with you, and she says she asks that you forgive her." This will only escalate your friend's anger. Second, why now? Waiting or postponing the ask for forgiveness only compounds the problem. The longer you wait, the more time you give the other person to distance themselves from you. Third, what will it do? Your ultimate goals when you ask for forgiveness are that you mend the relationship, put this unfortunate incident behind you, return to the positive relationship, and move forward.

If this all appears to be logical and simple, why don't we go through these steps and move on? Because for many of us, asking ourselves to apologize is an admission that we did something wrong, and that leaves us vulnerable. It can be extremely difficult to take a direct and honest approach and be responsible for our actions and our words. Throughout this book I have emphasized the winning and now healing effects of putting structure into your asks. If you can detach your emotions for just a bit and ask and then answer these three questions, your asks of yourself will be a whole lot easier and very rewarding for your relationships.

Let's see how the 5-Step Foolproof Method for Any Ask can help us with asks for ourselves. Step 1 is *to know exactly what you want*, including numbers and dates. What you want is to be forgiven and to have no hard feelings between you and the person who was hurt. As I've stated and as I'm sure you know, the longer you wait, the better the chance that the person who was hurt will be less and less forgiving. So I suggest that you put a date on this ask as soon as you can, like the day or two after the incident occurred. Think of how many family issues could be resolved if we just applied this simple step. Step 2 is *to prepare the conversation*. Here is where you need to write down all the responses you think the person will say. Your ask for forgiveness could be, "Jesse, I'm very sorry I shouted at you; I let my anger get the best of me. I apologize, and I ask that you forgive me. Can we put this behind us now?" Now let's write down everything we think Jesse might reply to your ask:

- "I've never before seen you so angry."
- "I can't just put this behind us."
- "You hurt me pretty badly."
- "What got into you?"
- "There must be more to this. What are you really upset about?"
- "I was wondering what you were going to do after your tirade."
- "I need some time to get over this."
- "Are you like this with other people, or am I the only lucky one?"
- "We've been friends for years. I would never do something like this to you."

You can add to this list, but it's a pretty good one to get you started. I started this chapter stating that asking for yourself is the same as any other ask *except for the soul-searching preparation part*. I believe this part is very emotional and it would be easy to skip it, just get it over with, or ignore that you need to ask and move on. But if you do spend your time preparing as you would for any other ask, I know you will be paving your way to an easier, less emotional ask experience.

Step 3 is *deliver with confidence.* When you ask for yourself, this has to focus on how you look and sound. Remember, this step requires strong eye contact and positive body language. It is natural to want to look down, look away, and turn inward, especially when asking someone to forgive you. After all, someone got hurt, and that does not lead to feeling upbeat and positive. I do not want you to be insincere or go overboard on being happy and effervescent, but be careful not to let the apology dampen the need for direct eye contact and body language.

Step 4, *clarify what you think you heard,* can get lost because emotions are running at an all-time high. Just look over the responses that Jesse gave to the person's ask for forgiveness. They range from trying to understand why the person offended him to trying to figure out how and when he will recover from the argument. Here is where clarifying what you think you heard reaches new heights. Here are ways you can clarify what you think you heard:

> **"I've never seen you so angry."**
> *"I agree. I haven't been this angry in a long time. I'm over it now, and I hope you are too. Can we agree that we will both move past this now?"*

> **"I can't just put this behind us."**
> *"I can understand that you can't put it behind you. You need more time. Can you tell me exactly what it is you can't put behind you? I want to help you in any way I can."*

> **"You hurt me pretty badly."**
> *"Again, I am truly sorry about what has happened. I can't take it back. But what I can do is help you now. What do you need from me?"*

> **"What got into you?"**
> *"Sometimes I'm caught off guard. Sometimes things just get to me, and this was unfair to you. I apologize. Can we agree to move through and beyond this?"*

> **"There must be more to this. What are you really upset about?"**
> *"Honestly, there isn't. It was just a bad day and a bad time. We are still good friends, right?"*

> **"I was wondering what you were going to do after your tirade."**
> *Actually, I was going to do nothing. I vented, I'm over it, and I apologize. Is there anything I can do to convince you this won't happen again?*

"I need some time to get over this."

"I've heard what you said. Yes, take as much time as you need. Please know I am here whether you want to talk or not. Is that OK with you?"

"Are you like this with other people, or am I the only lucky one!"

"Funny you should mention luck and anger. I'm so sorry, but I guess I take my anger out on the people I am closest to. I promise I will do my best not to take this out on you any more, OK?"

"We've been friends for years. I would never do something like this to you."

"You have every right to feel upset, and yes, we have been friends for years. This is on me 100 percent. I will do my best not to have this happen again, OK?"

This is really the best you can do to respond to their concerns. Remember it's about *them* not you when you are in these situations, so use the examples I've given, insert your own language, and speak from the heart. Above all keep it short; *two sentences and a question* will serve you well here.

Step 5, *plan your next move at the ask*, should be an easy task, but let's make sure you don't skip over this. You could say something like:

"I'm really grateful for your understanding. Friends like you are rare, and I don't take that for granted. How about we meet for breakfast on me next week?"

"Take all the time you need. I'm here. Would it be OK if I called just to check in with you next Tuesday at 7:00 PM?"

"I understand that you need more time. May I stop by in two weeks just to see how you are and what I can do?

I'm sure you are saying to yourself that all this takes way too much time and that you will never do any of this. Still, look deep into the steps I've outlined. Whether you apply the three questions or the five steps, it will save you a lot of time and emotional energy. Don't you wish at some point you had used these simple phrases I've outlined to mend some really hard situations that caused you stress and left you emotionally spent? Simple asks lead to simple solutions. Try it. It works, and it will work for you.

LAURA'S STORY—THE HARDEST ASKS
I HAVE EVER MADE

I would never ask you to do something or take an emotional journey unless I was willing to do it myself. I do practice what I preach, and I have preached in this book that if you make any ask, you should be prepared to be asked back. So I want to end this book (and endings can be very difficult), with an experience I had recently that actually motivated me to write this book. Read on, and you will see how this all comes together. Asks are not just about money or having someone do something for you. Asks are also what you need to do for yourself—what *you and only you* can do for yourself. That is why it is so important for your personal and professional growth that you focus on the asks you need to make of yourself.

I came to a point in my career when I felt stuck, really stuck. I had written the first two books on THE ASK, and despite their titles: *THE ASK: How to ASK Anyone for Any Amount for Any Purpose* and *THE ASK: How to ASK for Your Nonprofit Cause, Creative Project, or Business Venture*, my readers knew me and knew my work in philanthropy. They applied what I had written only to charitable causes and raising philanthropic dollars. Somehow they skipped over the "Creative Project" and "Business Venture" parts of the books. People would walk up to me and ask me how they could get the bank to give them a better rate on a loan, how to get people to finance their new play, how to ask for increased or repeat business, how to ask their children to get a job, or how to ask a parent to consider moving into an assisted-living facility? It was maddening to me because I would say, "It's in the book!" Alas, they thought it applied only to nonprofits. I was on a quest for quite some time to show the world that The ASK applies everywhere and in every situation. Even when I was speaking on The ASK internationally I would always say, "What you are about to hear applies whether you are raising money for charity, raising money for your business, or raising a family," but somehow it would be taken to refer only to helping nonprofits.

I had a few choices I could make. I could continue helping nonprofits everywhere to take their fundraising programs to exciting new levels and be happy with my work, or I could pursue my goals. I chose the latter—surprise, surprise. My first goal was to get the message out that THE ASK applies to everything and on every level. I knew that I needed outside help and had to admit that I could not do this on my own despite my years of speaking and writing books on this very topic. I asked friends and colleagues and even went to networking sessions on how to build a business, given that I was in fact building a brand-new business—THE ASK for everyone. Getting outside the world of nonprofits and into the business and lifestyle area was completely new to me and represented a brand-new business.

I decided at first to hire a public relations firm to help me get the word out about THE ASK. I thought what better place than the media to be known as *the* person when it comes to asking for anything. Soon I was on national network television and radio stations talking about "Questions You Don't ASK Your Doctor that Cost You Money," "How to ASK for Exactly What You Want on Valentine's Day," and "How to ASK for a Divorce." (I would have preferred to talk about "How to ASK Someone to Marry You," but I wasn't the interviewer.) I hit the big time when I landed an interview on America's Headline News on "How political candidates can ASK for the big bucks for their campaigns." I was quoted quite frequently in the *New York Times* and the *Wall Street Journal* on topics ranging from "How financial planners can ASK their clients for donor-advised funds" to "How to ASK celebrities to do more with your organization." Things were going really well, but once you are on or in the news, then what? It still was not getting through that THE ASK needed a bigger platform and a more ongoing presence. My public relations firm knew it too. They said they had taken me as far as they could and recommended that I speak with Daniella Cracknell, CEO and founder of Leonard George, an international reputation development company for entrepreneurs, philanthropists, and creatives. Daniella was an expert in reputation building, and that's what her company does; it builds reputations primarily with celebrities. I was not a celebrity (yet), and I thought my reputation was just fine so I really didn't see where this was going.

I explained to Daniella that I wanted to achieve my first goal: getting THE ASK beyond philanthropy and into business and everyday living and that now I had an additional goal. I wanted my own television show! That's right, I wanted a regular show that people could watch each day as I tackled their ask problems on health, fashion, travel, religion, relationships, beauty, careers, weddings, parenting, retirement, creativity, spirituality, and fun. After watching endless episodes of *The Nonprofit*, *Oprah*, *Dr. Phil*, *Dr. Oz*, *The Steve Harvey Show*, *The Doctors*, and *The Millionaire Matchmaker* and listening to call-in radio shows across the country, I knew that THE ASK could help millions of people. Most of the problems and issues boiled down to one thing: People were living miserable or compromised lives because they could not ask. They stayed in miserable relationships because they wouldn't ask for something they needed in the relationship. They were intimidated or fearful to ask their doctor probing questions or for alternatives to the doctor's advice. They resented their work because they were not being paid what they were worth. They resented their boss for not appreciating their work. I found myself writing down everything they should be asking for on these shows using the exact words, and at that moment I said to myself, "I need my own show."

Daniella listened to what I wanted but explained that the hurdles would be great. I wasn't 20 or 30 years of age, and that's what sells in the media. I thought to myself that at 20 or 30 years of age, I could not possibly have known what I know now. I hadn't experienced enough of life and challenging situations or practiced my asks, so how could I have asked for a show much earlier in life? That wasn't going to deter me. Next she laid out the timeline and her fees for what it would take to get The ASK into everyday living.

Then it happened. I was faced with the first and hardest ask I had to make of myself: "*Could I put my dreams first and invest in me?*" This was going to be a major investment, and I knew it—an investment of time and an investment of a lot of money. Then my money blockers came marching in. I can't tell you how many conversations I had in my head, the lists and edits of my pros and cons, and the back-and-forth I went through to reach this decision. "Is it worth it?" "Should I have done this years ago, and is it too late now?" "I'm about to wipe out an entire savings account; is that a smart thing to do?" "There are no guarantees. What if I do it, get nothing, and then have less for my retirement?" That's just a few of the dozens of questions that swirled in my head. The hardest part was to push away these fears, believe in myself and my dream, and answer my difficult ask: "*Could I put my dreams first and invest in me?*" After a spending a lot of mental and emotional energy and second guessing, I did it. I said to myself, "I'm worth it; let's do this!"

Daniella read everything I had written, all my books and numerous articles in the philanthropic, business and lifestyle publications and everything written about me. It surprised me how much media coverage I received over these years. When she was finished she said you are now "The Expert on The ASK." A reputation was born—mine—and there was no turning back. Everything had to be aligned and consistent with my new brand. I had The ASK logo, The ASK tagline, "May Every Ask Be Your Best Ask," a new website that featured how to ask for philanthropy, business, and everyday living (www.expertontheask.com). Even my physical appearance had to change. On Daniella's suggestion I hired a stylist, Andy Paige, who came to my house and literally discarded every piece of clothing I had, except for maybe 11 garments. Talk about a purge! My clothes were too business-like and in all the wrong colors. Andy shopped with me for two solid days from 9:00 AM until 9:00 PM until we had everything aligned with my brand. My clothes were now vibrant blues and greens to match my logo and the assorted jewel-tone colors that pop up on television and social media. We bought all new shoes, underwear, makeup, and jewelry. The third day I got a brand-new hair style and all new headshots that visually delivered with confidence that I was ready for my show and that this is what The ASK looks like. All these physical enhancements represented additional investments as you can imagine, but by now I was on a roll and there was no looking back and certainly no quitting.

My speaking engagements and media appearances were transformed because I myself was transformed, physically and emotionally. I found myself dropping the nonprofit speak and getting into the lifestyle language. That was the piece that had been missing and that I could not figure out for myself. Although in my head I said that I was speaking differently to audiences and not boxing myself into nonprofit lingo, I really wasn't. My previous talks hadn't conveyed enough emotion, enough heart, and enough of my learning from my mistakes. I will never forget the time at the end of one of my speaking engagements a man came up to me and said, "But Laura, we aren't you and we can't be like you because you know how to ask so perfectly." I thought to myself, this man and my audiences have no idea how many mistakes I made and it was through those mistakes that I learned how to make the right ask. Then it dawned on me that I had never shared my mistakes and how I corrected them to get me to this point in my life. From that moment on, I made sure in every presentation I said, "And I'm sharing all of this with you because I made these mistakes." That simple adjustment that I was just like everyone else who needed to ask and figured out a system how anyone could ask made all the difference in the world. My previous talks hadn't shared enough stories or shown how ordinary or extraordinary people of any age living anywhere could use these simple steps and get their lives back on track. Now, armed with a new brand, a new look, and a new awareness of what THE ASK could do for anyone who needed it, I was ready to showcase THE ASK to mainstay audiences and to find the right developer for my show.

Or so I thought. Time was passing by, and even though I had speaking engagements for business and lifestyle audiences, I still didn't have my show. I stepped back to reassess, and I asked myself, "Why isn't this happening?" Then it dawned on me: Was I really ready for all this? Everything was changing, could I handle it? And then I made the second hardest ask of myself. I asked myself "*Could I handle success when it comes my way?*" That ask went deep, very deep. My answer was that of course I could, but I was fooling myself. All the self-doubt, all the "this is just a fantasy, it will never happen" came creeping in. I never realized I had so many sabotaging thoughts and ways to end what I had started, what I had invested in. Thoughts came in like "I'm not getting any younger," "Social media has changed everything," "No one is doing a talk or a panel talk show anymore," and "If it hasn't happened by now, it never would." That was the way I masked my fear of success.

So again I went back to where I started and remembered that whenever I could not do something for myself, I needed to ask for outside help. This was the third hardest ask I have made of myself: "*Who could I trust to help me accept success when it comes?*" This is a huge ask for me, and I'm sure I'm not alone when it comes to hesitating to ask for help and trusting someone to help me. I really didn't know who would be the right person to help me get through and beyond this fear of success. After all, if you are a strong personality, as I am, and you are used to acting pretty independently, it takes a lot of commitment to put your trust and faith into another person or entity.

I must say that I did not go around asking for this kind of help, because I thought it sounded really silly. Besides, how do you frame that kind of ask? I didn't know how, so I didn't, and I kept it to myself. To my good fortune I had a colleague who was in a side business with me who had just come back from a Tony Robbins conference. Many of you may know that Tony is charismatic life coach who speaks around the world transforming people's approaches to relationships, money, careers, leadership and health. His conferences attract thousands and he is a well-known author as well. My colleague had had an incredible experience and in fact was going to do Tony's session "Unleash the Power Within" for a second time that July in Chicago. She said that I should go because it would help me be better at my business. At first I thought the timing was bad since it would be in the summer and I needed some time off. I had heard that Tony gets thousands of people at his conferences and that on the first night he makes you walk on fire. Did I really want to walk on fire? What could he do for me? Then I thought, "He has helped so many people around the world, so why don't I give it a shot? At the very least I would come back with a positive thought or two that could help me." So off to Chicago I went.

To no one's surprise, I put myself through the five steps. I wanted to walk away at the end of the conference feeling 100 percent that I deserved the successes that I knew I wanted and were coming my way. I did my preparation by listing all the negative thoughts I had about why those successes would not or might not come and reversed them into positive affirmations. I asked myself whether I'd be willing to accept the remarkable successes that I was about to receive and answered, "You bet I am." I showed up at the conference each morning one hour before it started, and gave it my all. Each night when I went back to my hotel I reiterated my own responses: "Yes I can," "I'm up for this," and "I have what it takes to be accepting of everything that comes my way." I even walked on fire that first night, and it did wonders to release my inner fears that I had carried with me for so many years. At the end of the conference I made an agreement with myself to read and re-read the material we were given. I also promised myself that I would take a long walk at least once a week and listen to his motivational tapes that would reinforce the certainty that I was ready to meet success head on.

I must share that I have never cried so hard in my adult life as I did at this conference. When I let everything go, I felt totally exposed and extremely vulnerable, but then it all lifted. When I recalled the expression "you carry the weight of the world on your shoulders" my shoulders going in felt like concrete cinder blocks but then became unbelievably light. It shocked me deeply that I would have such a hard time with something so wonderful. After all, doesn't everyone want success? And when it comes, do you say, "No, thank you?" But it was tremendously difficult for me, and that was a very precious and excruciatingly difficult ask. "*Could I accept success when it comes my way?*" has been one of the hardest asks I have ever had to make of myself to date.

Armed with an abundance of renewed confidence, faith, and commitment to myself that I deserved every success, I took my first goal of getting THE ASK into business and mainstream audiences to new levels. I starting attracting major corporate clients to train their sales forces on how to ask for business and repeat business. National lifestyle magazines, major business journals, online news agencies, and radio and blog-post commentaries all asked for my asking advice on topics such as cosmetic surgery, weddings, parenting, saving the elephants, politics, and wellness. My article on "How to ASK for a destination wedding" landed on the cover of *Bridal Guide!* Since wellness was and continues to be a hot topic for people of every generation, I created a 30-Day Money Wellness program, where your health is your wealth, and wrote an e-book, *Money Wellness: Is Money Making You $ick?* I followed that with a program I designed called the *7-Day Guide to Money and Your Significant Other.* Both are available on my website (www.expertontheask .com). Now I became the THE ASK healer for physical and mental health and relationships. I was THRILLED!

But in the back of my head was that lingering thought, that constant reminder, that I didn't have my show. THE ASK was certainly getting more popular and gaining more traction with broader audiences, but I still didn't have that outreach on a consistent basis that a show can bring. Well, I got lucky again, *very* lucky. I say there are angels everywhere, and this one was looking down at me and saying, "Yeah—she's ready!"

A conference, "Speak Up Women," was being held at the United Nations and the organizer of the conference asked me to be on a panel to talk about how women can speak up for themselves when it comes to their finances. I was covering how to ASK for money for your business and your life, and my fellow panelists were speaking about how to raise money through crowdfunding and how to attract a venture capitalist to invest in your business. When it came time for the question-and-answer period, a woman way in the back of the room asked a question I had never heard before: "How do I know whom to accept money from and in what order for my business?"

Well that got my attention, and before anyone on the panel could speak, I jumped off my chair and said quite loudly, "I've got this one. I have got to answer this one or I will fly out of this room." So I first asked her whether this group of potential funders included one person or several people that she knew, liked, and trusted. She said, "Of course," but some people had approached her first who were not in that category and there were others who could invest more but were not in that category. I explained to her that she should want to invest with people that she trusted as lifelong partners. These would be people she could learn from and grow with. Unless she knew, liked, and trusted them, all the money in the world would not matter. Her business would not grow, because there would be no solid bond of trust. When it comes to money, there has to be trust. Without trust, she would be right back at square one.

The conference ended and we all gathered at a hotel for a cocktail reception. It is a rare occasion when I would sit down at a reception, because I like to mingle and hear people's thoughts about the day. I love to hear what they learned and often ask, "What is the one thing you know now that you did not know at 9:00 AM this morning?" That lets me know what has resonated with each person and what they will take home and apply. Since I had been up since 5:00 AM preparing for this panel, I was tired. So I sat down and just started looking around the room and listening to peoples' conversations. Then a woman sat down at my table, looked me straight in the eyes, and said, "Laura, what do you want?" I thought, "What do I want! What do you mean what do I want, and I don't even know this person." Before I answered, it dawned on me that this was the woman in my session who had asked that stellar question I had to answer: "How do I know whom to accept money from and in what order for my business?" So I said, "Oh you asked that question. I loved that question." Then I asked her, "Do you really want to know what I want?" She said, "Yes" and nothing more. Not why she wanted to know. That was it.

So I shared with her exactly what I wanted in graphic detail. I told her I wanted my own show and it would be called *The Nonprofit*. My show would be about my going into nonprofits and turning them around. It would be about mission, motivation, and money. The shows I designed would change with each episode. How could a celebrity become more engaged with a nonprofit so that the nonprofit could raise more money rather than just providing the occasional presence at a special event that many celebrities offer? When a charity experiences a tragic sudden loss of funds, what could I do to jumpstart funding? If the charity was burdened with some really bad publicity that caused donors to leave or board members to quit, what could I do to get back donor confidence? If an international charity wants to attract United States donors, how could I explain that U.S. donors invariably need a personal relationship or a connection to the charity before they will give? I had dozens of episodes mapped out that would attract a variety of audiences worldwide. Audience members would have the opportunity to support that charity online or give to the charity directly at the end of each show. I even had the episodes that would look back, a sort of "Where are they now?" show to see how the charity was doing after that show had ended. Best of all, I knew I was the right person for the show and that no one to date owned the space in the media to showcase nonprofits. I had to have this.

After my extensive explanation of what I wanted, the woman who sat down next to me at the reception said, "I can do that." I thought, "You can do this? Who are you?" So I asked her, "What's your name and what do you do?" She said, "I'm Jenevieve Brewer, and I have my own talent-management company, and you would be perfect for a show like that." I was stunned. At first I thought she was joking with me. To be sure I asked her to explain what she does and how she got to the point of owning her own talent agency. After she laid out her extensive background of initially writing for television shows and television publications and then becoming entrenched with finding and placing new talent for new shows, I was convinced she was the real deal and that she could help me. More important, I really liked her. She was younger than me and had accomplished so much. She was that "old soul in a very young body." Having done my work to get to this point, because now I could trust someone to help me achieve my success I looked her straight in the eyes and said, "Great; let's make this happen!"

Over the next several months, Jenevieve and I talked and met every week. Since we had the concept for the show, our next step was to find a production company. This was not an easy task because I'm not a known talent, I'm not a young talent, and our show concept was brand new. While Jenevieve was working her connections, I had to work mine. So I turned to my board of directors. I am part of a group of women. We call each other our "board of directors," and we meet every four months to see how we can help each other out. I love it because it is right up my alley. We go around the room, and we can each make one ask. We ask for something that we need, and then we each see whether we know someone or have a connection for them.

My ask at the meeting was for a connection to a production company that would be interested in producing our show. As luck would have it, one woman at the meeting knew of a production company and offered to make the introduction for me. Just one month later, Jenevieve and I met with that production company. They loved our idea, and we were on our way to developing the show. My dream and my quest had all come together. If I had not had the courage to make the hard asks of myself, work through and beyond the money blockers, and do some very serious soul-searching as to whether I deserved all that was about to come to me, none of this would never have materialized.

As of the writing of this book, the story gets better. The initial idea to have me featured in the show *The Nonprofit* is on hold because we have something even better. While we were discussing all the possible episodes that could be in this show our development team became fascinated in what I knew about nonprofits, where I predicted large gifts would be targeted, how millennials would respond to volunteering, and how nonprofits would have a larger role. I've been in this field for 25+ years so I have a really good handle on the subject, but more importantly, they saw my talent for much more. They saw that I could critique a money pitch, since I know what motivates people to give, and refine it so that either an entrepreneur or philanthropist would be really interested in investing. They also saw that I know how people with millions and billions will or will not be inspired to give, since I have personally asked and coached people to do so.

So as I write, we are working on a show much like the show *Shark Tank*, where I will critique entrepreneurs' pitches for new ideas, products, or techniques to clean our oceans and then advise our potential billionaire investors if they should make that investment, partner with nonprofits, or save their money for a future deal. Imagine that! That is just the beginning. We plan to expand the show by inviting world-renowned marine biologists and other experts who could weigh in and help me advise our billionaires if the entrepreneurs' ideas are worthy of investment. I feel beyond elated that I did my work, as torturous and as painful as it was to take the time and get my answer to the question, "*Could I accept success when it comes my way?*" Armed with my excellent and extraordinarily talented team around me, I have 100 percent confidence that a show is forthcoming. I want this, I deserve this, and I am so ready to accept it when it comes. THE ASK got me here, and believe me, there is no stopping me now.

I do hope my story, my journey, and my hard asks of myself have inspired and will inspire and motivate you to make those hard asks of yourself. Trust me—they are not easy or comfortable, and you will cry a lot or beat yourself up with your negative thoughts. But if you devote the time and focus on the energies you will need for working through and beyond your stumbling blocks and the money blockers that are preventing you from having all that you deserve and all that you want, you will prevail. You are worth it. You deserve it. Make those hard asks of yourself. My money's on you, and I'm with you all the way!

Conclusion

IT IS MY SINCERE WISH THAT BY NOW YOU see that THE ASK is much more than you imagined. THE ASK is about *empowerment, personal pride, momentum, possibilities,* and *self-improvement.* It takes organization, structure, and focus to make those exceptional asks as well as to put yourself first and make the hard asks of yourself. You know how to recognize your money blockers and work through and beyond them so they do not get in the way of your asks. You also know the many reasons why people don't ask, but that will not stop you from asking, because you now know the actions you need to take before you ask. Anyone can be that exceptional asker if they carefully go through the checklist of 10 characteristics of the exceptional asker. The three questions before each ask as well as the 5-Step Foolproof Method for Any Ask will serve you well as long as you keep practicing those techniques. They take time, but they will bring you the results you want once you incorporate them into every daily aspect of your life. My asking mantras will get you through each and every ask you need to make, but please add your own and say them to yourself every time you need to make that important ask.

You now have *over 175 ways*, as presented in this book, that you can use to ask for anything you want. Think of them as puzzle pieces. You can select the ones you want, use my proposed words or chose your own. The point is to first see how they can fit for you and adapt for your particular ask. Just remember to make your ask *two sentences and a question*. This simple concept will bring you transformational successes time and time again. It will also prevent you from over-asking your ask and ensuring that you speak at most 25 percent of the time and the person you are asking speaks 75 percent of the time.

Hearing a no to your ask or catching your asking mistakes will no longer be a deterrent for you. You can turn any response into an ask win. Carefully go over your words and determine if your ask was really an ask or was it a statement? Your ultimate goal for any response other than a yes is to find out why. Why can't this person do what you asked? Once you are in sync and have a total and complete understanding as to what they are thinking or what is preventing them from giving you an immediate yes, you can proceed on the same path and work it out together. You now know that the ask has no room for assumptions or fill-in-the-blank guessing otherwise you will walk away empty handed and dis-appointed. The worst is that last empty experience will make you hesitate the next time to ask.

The ask is a group hug, keep the person you are asking close to you and always ask, "How can we work this out together?" This way they do not feel alone, under a spotlight or microscope, forced to make a quick judgment. If you thought long and hard about what you want, why you want it and why you want it now you will be in that position to work anything out to your satisfaction.

Honesty wins the day and if you have no idea if the person can do what you are about to ask for then say it: "I honestly have no idea if you can do this but it is so important to me." Short, simple, to the point, and loaded with genuine honesty. People will be more attracted to you and your ask when you are honest, so let that come through each and every time you ask.

To recap, with all the organization, structure, and focus in the world, you now have everything you need to be that exceptional asker.

THE ASK is your new way of approaching life.

THE ASK will guide your life experiences.

THE ASK will help you get the things you want, desire, and deserve.

THE ASK can help anyone at any age for any purpose.

THE ASK is endlessly rewarding.

I leave you with my Top 10 Best ASKing tips, one from each chapter:

1. *Money is opportunity*—embrace it, make it your mantra, and push away any other thought that comes creeping in and sets you up for doubt and failure.
2. The quality of your life is determined by the *quality of the questions you ask yourself and others.*
3. Whenever you ask, you should be *100 percent committed*, with absolute certainty that this is what you want for your organization, your business, your personal growth, and your happiness.
4. *People leave clues*, and we miss every one of them.
5. THE ASK—*it's two sentences and a question.*
6. *Don't assume* that since you deserve it you don't have to ask for it.
7. Your ask will go well if the person you are asking *knows, likes, and trusts you.*
8. "May we be *your next largest investment?*" is a great ask.
9. Keep it simple; *don't over-ask your ask.*
10. The most difficult yet rewarding asks are the ones *you ask of yourself.*

Now go for the life you know you want. THE ASK will undoubtedly get you there. May every ASK be your best ASK!

About the Author

L AURA FREDRICKS, BASED IN NEW YORK City, is the billion-dollar ask-maker powerhouse, who, as CEO and founder of THE A$K, trains and coaches nonprofits and businesses on how to ask for money—and more of it. She is the first to combine the most trusted professions—law and philanthropy— to show how any person, charity, or business can raise money in unprecedented levels. For over 25 years, she has advised organizations around the globe on current trends within the philanthropic world and has shared her thoughts on the management of their assets, personnel, and organizational structure. Her five books, including *THE ASK*, are the international industry-leading, go-to guides. She is today's money wellness expert and has become a media personality.

As an attorney-turned-philanthropic advisor, Laura Fredricks knows how to ask. She comes from a seasoned career in industries best known for making the most high-profile asks—law and philanthropy—and is the first to merge strategies from both professional sectors into a mainstream practice now known as THE ASK, also available for the business and consumer lifestyle marketplace. This new practice has placed Laura on the national and international speaking circuits and at conferences around the world from Amsterdam to Annapolis, Bologna to Boca Raton, Moscow to Madison, Sydney to Seattle, and Vancouver to Vail.

THE ASK has also led her to TV and radio appearances on national and local talk shows, and her expertise has been featured in national publications.

MONEY WELLNESS EXPERT

Laura is the "money wellness expert" with an all-new, 30-day on-line money wellness program. Her book *Money Wellness: Is Money Making You $ick?* is the first to explore how money affects your diet, sleep, exercise, spirituality, creativity, and fun, and it tells you how you can work out your *money blockers* that prevent you from having the best relationship with money. Laura's "Seven Days to Money and Your Significant Other" online program has helped couples work out their money issues so they can get back to romance.

IVY LEAGUE LECTURER

In addition to her philanthropy work, Laura Fredricks has taught nonprofit business management and fundraising techniques at Columbia University, New York University, Duke University, University of Pennsylvania, The Smithsonian Institute, and the Harvard and Princeton Clubs. Her courses cover nonprofit leadership, fundraising trends, and how to ask for major, planned, special events, and capital campaign gifts. She has been teaching since 1994 and is a current advisory board member for New York University and Columbia University's fundraising programs.

FUNDRAISING TRACK RECORD

Laura Fredricks entered the fundraising field serving as the Philadelphia Bar Foundation's director of development, where she launched a major gifts program that increased individual giving by more than 75 percent. As vice president for philanthropy at Pace University in New York City, she was the driving force behind an unprecedented $100 million charitable raise during a six-year campaign period right after the 9/11 terrorist attacks. In this role, she oversaw all aspects of fundraising and alumni relations for a staff of 40 across five state-wide campuses.

Prior to her tenure at Pace, Laura Fredricks was associate vice president for development at Philadelphia's Temple University, where she managed and coordinated major and planned giving programs, corporate and foundation funding, and alumni relations for 15 schools and colleges, two hospitals, and the athletic program during a $300 million campaign. As major gifts manager for the Deborah Hospital Foundation, she elevated the major gift program from $50,000 to $6.1 million from grateful patients in just one year.

In addition to her contributions to academic boards, Laura Fredricks has served as an executive board member for the Association of Fundraising Professionals (AFP) Greater New York Chapter; AFP Philadelphia; Operation Homefront, which supports military families; and for the Cherry Lane Theatre, the oldest, continuously running off-Broadway theatrical house. In addition, Laura has been a longtime volunteer with Big Brothers, Big Sisters of America.

MEDIA EXPERT

Laura Fredricks was most recently interviewed on CNN speaking on the impact of a possible $500 million federal funding cut for Planned Parenthood and she has also appeared on Fox's *America's Headline News,* commenting on how presidential candidates should ask for money. As "The Expert on THE ASK" she provided Katie Couric and her ABC News/Yahoo News viewers with tips on how to ask for what you want.

Laura's asking strategies for better living have also found themselves on the pages of popular lifestyle publications such as *The Huffington Post, Women's Health, Shape, Self,* and *The Bridal Guide,* as well as in major-market newspapers. The *Chicago Tribune* featured her "easy-to-please asking tactics" that deliver "how to get exactly what you want (or don't want!) on Valentine's Day." Her tips, tools, and best practices can be used and applied instantly to any facet of everyday life, at any time, from anywhere—in relationships, finance, health, and careers. Her "asking advice for everyday living" has also become a topic for TV segments on local talk shows across the nation.

Listeners to radio programs on New York's WOR, Chicago's WGN, and Sirius XM Satellite Radio have also been benefitting from Laura's motivational voice with tips on how to ask for travel upgrades and questions you are not asking your doctor that could cost you money.

In the corporate sector, Laura's *financial asking philosophies* have been featured in *The Wall Street Journal, The New York Times,* and *Financial Advisor IQ,* as well as on WSJ Live: Dow Jones Wealth Advisor. She has provided entrepreneurs with tips on how to snag a superstar client simply by knowing how to ASK for them. She has also been quoted throughout the philanthropic community in *The Chronicle of Philanthropy* and *Advancing Philanthropy.*

To keep energy and focus up and at all times, Laura mountaineers through the high peaks of the Adirondack Mountains. For more about Laura, please visit www.expertontheask.com.

Index